TO THE PAST:
HISTORY EDUCATION, PUBLIC MEMORY,
AND CITIZENSHIP IN CANADA

Recent years have witnessed a breakdown in consensus about the history taught in Canadian schools as a heightened awareness has developed of the political nature of deciding whose history is, or should be, included in social studies and history classrooms. Meanwhile, as educators are debating what should be taught, developments in educational and cognitive research are expanding our understanding of how best to teach it. *To the Past* explores some of the political, cultural, and educational issues surrounding the study of history, and why we should care about it, in the twenty-first century in Canada.

Originally broadcast on the CBC Radio program *Ideas*, the lectures that constitute this volume not only address how and what history is taught, but also explore strands within larger discussions about the meaning and purposes of history more generally. Contributors suggest that Canadians are demonstrating a new interest in what scholars have termed 'historical consciousness' or collective memory, through participation in a wide range of cultural activities, from visiting museums to watching the History Channel. Adults and children alike seem to be seeking answers to questions of identity, meaning, community, and nation in their study of the past and *To the Past* raises some of the political and ethical issues involved in this emerging field of 'citizenship through history.'

RUTH SANDWELL is an assistant professor in the Department of Theory and Policy Studies at the Ontario Institute for Studies in Education of the University of Toronto.

To the Past

History Education, Public Memory, and Citizenship in Canada

Edited by Ruth W. Sandwell

UNIVERSITY OF TORONTO PRESS
Toronto Buffalo London

© University of Toronto Press Incorporated 2006
Toronto Buffalo London
Printed in Canada

ISBN 0-8020-3891-3 (cloth)
ISBN 0-8020-3814-X (paper)

Printed on acid-free paper

Library and Archives Canada Cataloguing in Publication

To the past : history education, public memory, and citizenship in
Canada / edited by Ruth Sandwell.

Includes bibliographical references.
ISBN 0-8020-3891-3 (bound)
ISBN 0-8020-3814-X (pbk.)

1. History – Study and teaching – Canada.   2. Canada – History.
I. Sandwell, R. W. (Ruth Wells), 1955–

FC155.T65 2006   971.0071   C2006-902225-9

University of Toronto Press acknowledges the financial assistance to
its publishing program of the Canada Council for the Arts and the
Ontario Arts Council.

University of Toronto Press acknowledges the financial support for
its publishing activities of the Government of Canada through the
Book Publishing Industry Development Program (BPIDP).

Contents

Contributors

Keith C. Barton is a professor in the Division of Teacher Education at the University of Cincinnati and has been a visiting professor in the UNESCO Programme in Education for Pluralism, Human Rights, and Democracy at the University of Ulster. He has conducted numerous studies of children's historical understanding in the United States and Northern Ireland, and he is co-author, with Linda S. Levstik, of *Teaching History for the Common Good* (2004) and *Doing History: Investigating with Children in Elementary and Middle Schools* (2005).

Chad Gaffield is a professor of history and was the founding director of the Institute of Canadian Studies at the University of Ottawa, and has published extensively in the fields of Canadian educational, community and family history. He was the president of the Canadian Historical Association in 2001. He is the lead researcher in the Canadian Century Research Infrastructure (CCRI), one of the most comprehensive humanities and social science research projects ever undertaken in Canada. In 2002 he was named professor of the year at the University of Ottawa.

Jocelyn Létourneau holds, at Laval University, a Canada Research Chair in the History and Political Economy of Contemporary Quebec. A fellow of the Royal Society of Canada, he is also a member of the Institute for Advanced Study, Princeton, New Jersey. His most recent books are *A History for the Future: Rewriting Memory and Identity in Quebec* (2004), and *Le Québec, les Québécois: Un parcours historique* (2004).

Desmond Morton is an emeritus professor of history at McGill University. He was the founding director of the McGill Institute for the Study of Canada and principal of the University of Toronto's Mississauga campus. He is the author of forty books about political, military, and industrial relations history, including best-sellers like *A Short History of Canada*, and is a frequent columnist and radio commentator.

Ken Osborne was educated at the Universities of Oxford, Birmingham, and Manitoba. He taught history in a Winnipeg high school from 1961 to 1972, when he joined the staff of the Faculty of Education at the University of Manitoba. At the University of Manitoba he won awards for excellence in teaching, for scholarship, and for community service. In 1996 he was awarded a Prix Manitoba for his work in heritage education and in 1999 a 'Distinguished Educator' award from OISE/ University of Toronto. He is now a professor emeritus of the University of Manitoba. He has served as editor of the national journal the *History and Social Science Teacher* and of the *Manitoba Social Science Teacher*. He has been involved in a variety of history curriculum development projects, both locally and nationally, and has written extensively on the teaching and learning of history and the place of history in citizenship education.

Ruth W. Sandwell teaches in the history and teacher education programs at the Ontario Institute for Studies in Education of the University of Toronto. In addition to studying rural Canada and the history of the family, she is interested in the intersection of history education and public memory in contemporary Canada, and she has published a number of articles in the field of history education. Her most recent book is *Contesting Rural Space: Land Policy and Practices of Resettlement on Saltspring Island, 1859–1891* (2005). She is co-director of the history education website series Great Unsolved Mysteries in Canadian History (www.canadianmysteries.ca), and co-director of The History Education Network (THEN)/Histoire et Éducation en Réseau (HiER) (www.historyeducation.ca).

Peter Seixas is a professor, Canada Research Chair, and director of the Centre for the Study of Historical Consciousness at the University of British Columbia. After teaching in Vancouver secondary schools for fifteen years and earning a PhD in history, he embarked upon a program of research on young people's historical understanding, which has resulted in numerous publications and presentations. He is editor of and contributor to *Theorizing Historical Consciousness* (2004) and co-editor, with Peter Stearns and Sam Wineburg, of *Knowing, Teaching and Learning History: National and International Perspectives* (2000).

Timothy J. Stanley teaches anti-racism education and the social foundations of education in the Faculty of Education at the University of Ottawa. He is also cross-appointed to the Department of History, where he has teaches Canadian and Chinese history. His publications on turn-of-the-twentieth century anti-Chinese racism in British Columbia, on the history wars in Canada, and contemporary racist discourse have appeared in a number of edited collections and journals including the *Canadian Historical Review, Histoire sociale/Social History,* the *Journal of the Canadian Historical Association,* and *Discourse: Studies in the Cultural Politics of Education.* He is currently completing a manuscript tentatively titled, *The White Man's Land Revisited: Racism, Education, and the Invention of Chinese Canadians.*

TO THE PAST

Introduction: History Education, Public Memory, and Citizenship in Canada

RUTH W. SANDWELL

Have historians, educational bureaucrats, and teachers conspired to make Canadian history as boring and irrelevant as possible? So Jack Granatstein hinted almost ten years ago in his inflammatory *Who Killed Canadian History?* Unfortunately, the strongest argument against such a conspiracy theory is that these three groups stopped talking to each other a generation ago, about the same time they stopped being listened to by most Canadians who care about history. Thankfully, however, history education has been staging a comeback in recent years, inside as well as outside the classroom. Inflamed by Granatstein's diatribe, or just plain worried about the future of the past, many Canadians have experienced a heightened awareness of the problems associated with history and have asked key questions about the discipline: Whose history *counts?* What people, events, and issues get to be included in social studies and history classrooms? Who and what are left out? And who decides these things? In recent years, it is almost as if history – a deeper understanding of where we have come from -- has been opening up a contemplative space where Canadians can reflect on who 'we' really are and start discussing who we really want to be.

Canadians are not alone in developing a more urgent sense of the past in recent years. Like other peoples around the globalizing world, Canadians have witnessed a breakdown in consensus about what history should be taught within government-sponsored educational systems. Whose point of view of 'the facts' should be highlighted: The winners'? The losers'? Do we have a national history, and, if so, is it reflected in school history curricula across the country? If the coherent stories that used to make up The History of Canada are more conflicted and varied than they used to be, the happy ending promised by history-as-a-story-of-unending-progress has also been tarnished by some damning evidence about environmental damage and the systematic abrogation of human rights throughout the past century, just to cite a couple of examples.

As school boards and Ministries of Education across the country are debating what history should be taught in Canadian classrooms, investigators in educational and cognitive research are exploring (and changing their minds about) how people accomplish 'historical thinking.' Their findings are providing some hard evidence about the ineffectiveness of traditional methods of history education, while students confirm recent research findings by consistently nominating history and social studies as their most-hated school subjects.

The breakdown in consensus about the who, the what, and the how of school history has been a source of considerable anxiety over the past few years, anxiety that has spilled over into 'the why' of history education. While few would be surprised that professional educators are concerned that history has become a contested and politicized terrain, it is worth noting that debates about what to teach, how, and why are emerging as strands within larger discussions about the social and political purposes of history, discussions that are neither limited to the classroom nor defined exclusively by professionals. For over the past few years, adults and children throughout Canadian society seem to be seeking answers to deeper questions of identity, meaning, community, and nation in their study of the past. Canadians are demonstrating a new interest in what scholars have termed 'historical consciousness' or 'collective memory,' and are expressing this in a wide range of cultural activities, from visiting museums to watching the History Channel, from taking the Dominion Institute's Canada Day history quiz to talking about what – and who – is part of their provincial history curriculum.

Each of the seven essays in this book brings together what might be termed the two arenas of history in Canada: 1) history and social studies as school subjects, and 2) history as a kind of intellectual space, a platform on which to observe and discuss a deeply personalized, collective, and meaningful understanding of human social relations through time. Although the authors vary considerably in their focus and emphasis as well as their evaluation of school history, they all root their discussions of history education in the bigger questions of historical consciousness: Why do we as members of a society, as citizens of a nation-state, as individuals in a series of overlapping communities, as parents, and as children, care about history? Through this series of essays, readers will have the opportunity to explore some of the political, philosophical, and ethical issues involved in this emerging field of Canadian 'citizenship through history,' as they read about how memory and history combine, often uncomfortably, with history education in Canadian schools.

All of the essays in this book, with the exception of Ken Osborne's remarkable concluding chapter, were delivered as part of a public lecture series that I had the privilege to organize at McGill University in the spring of 2002. Indicating the general interest that issues of history education have been generating throughout Canadian society over the past few years, the Canadian Broadcasting Corporation's Radio One program *Ideas* recorded the series, broadcasting the lectures in the fall of 2002 and again in 2003. The essays in this collection, though all written by academic historians and history educators and published by a university press, are not directed at a narrowly academic or specialized audience. Instead, they are intended here, as they were in the public lecture series in which they were first delivered, to mend together the deep interest that Canadians have in their individual and collective pasts with the practices and research of historians, and with what is learned and taught in history classrooms. All are informed by the conviction that a knowledge of history is of profound significance to all Canadians.

The lecture series originated in an idea I had in the fall of 2001, shortly after I had arrived at McGill University to take up a unique joint appointment in history and education. Although I am a historian by training and inclination, by 2001 I had been working for some years as a history educator as well. On the side, as it were, I collaborated with a colleague at the University of Victoria (Dr John Lutz) to create a web-based history education project entitled the Great Unsolved Mysteries of Canadian History (www.canadianmysteries.ca). On the website, visitors are invited to solve a more or less unknown mystery in Canadian history by interpreting hundreds of historical documents provided on the web site. The surprising popularity of these mystery sites among high school history teachers and students across the continent had in turn brought me into contact with many history teachers and university history educators. By the summer of 2001, I had some claim to being both a historian and someone with knowledge and expertise in the practices of teaching history.

Even though I had read Granatstein's book in the late nineties, and had been thinking a lot about the problems he pointed to, it was not until I took up the joint position at McGill that I fully comprehended just how much 'the problem' of history education has been exacerbated by failures of communication. There is a tremendous gulf separating historians from other history educators in Canada, and another gulf separating school history both from what historians do and from the kinds of history that many Canadians care so much about. The breakdown in communication between professional historians and history educators, on the one hand, and between both these groups and non-teachers, on the other, has had some serious consequences for Canadian historical consciousness, as a number of the authors in this collection will argue. There are, furthermore, two clearly observable effects of the fracture in communication between historians and history teachers. Historians have remained largely unaware of changes in education that have, in some subject areas, been transforming teaching practices; and history teachers have, for the most part, remained largely unaware of important changes that have, over the past fifty years, transformed the ways that historians understand and approach the discipline. From the vantage point of elementary and secondary school history teachers, the work of professional historians in the post-1960 period has been increasingly 'academic' in the worst sense of the word: irrelevant, pretentious, and frequently unreadable. For historians, the work of history teachers has been seen as, at best, facile and irrelevant, and at its worst a more or less benign form of government propaganda. Regardless of which group was most to blame for the breakdown in communication, this gulf has, arguably, been at the heart of the decline of history as a school and university subject, and is probably related to the decline in Canadians' understanding of their collective cultural heritage. Canadians do not, for the most part, identify what they learn from either professional historians or from high school history teachers as meaningful history.

The public lecture series, entitled 'Public Memory, Citizenship, and History Education,' which doubled as part of a graduate course in history education in the spring of 2002, was my attempt to draw some attention to the problems of history education. The original lecture series, like this publication, builds on the pioneering work of Canada's National History Society, Historica, the Association of Canadian Studies, the McGill Institute for the Study of Canada, and the Centre for the Study of Historical Consciousness at the University of British Columbia to open up the dialogue between historians, history educators, and Canadians outside the fields of history or education. Historians and history educators need a common intellectual space to discuss and participate actively in the changes that have transformed history over the past half century and that are currently changing history education in other parts of the world. Historians themselves need to be brought into discussions about history education not simply as experts to advise teachers and history educators, but as teachers as well, teachers who can benefit greatly from discussions about the pedagogical issues that too often create insurmountable barriers between what they teach as university professors and what students learn about history. And Canadians as a whole, in all their complex diversity, have much to offer to and learn from the politics of memory that is, and should be, at the heart of history education in Canada.

In the first essay, Peter Seixas takes on the big question 'What is historical consciousness?' In the past decade, many of the calls for increased history in schools have arisen from concerns about Canadian identity and Canadian unity. Parents and teachers routinely ask the school history classroom to play a central role in shaping national collective memory. But these campaigns often underplay difficult challenges: How can teachers deal with complex historical issues of identity, difference, and community? Can they effectively bridge the divide that so often exists between families' personal or ethnic histories and the 'official' versions of textbook history? How should they respond to film and new media in shaping young people's historical understanding? Seixas's essay reviews some key recent research to define the field of 'historical consciousness' in relation to those of history, historiography, and collective memory. He concludes by arguing that there is an urgent need to revise and rethink our expectations of school history in the light of this research.

In chapter 2, well-known Canadian historian Desmond Morton suggests that the problems of imposing a standard Canadian public memory through provincially funded systems of education go back a long way, and they are not ours alone. Across Europe and in the United States, 'history wars' have been common. How odd, he argues, that historians so seldom use their craft to understand these issues. If they did, would they revisit old frustrations and repeat old mistakes? They might ask why students find lists of obligatory facts unmemorable. They might measure the ratio of teaching to learning. They might ask whose agenda school history serves. Is history, like youth, wasted on the young? Could history become a powerful tool for understanding ourselves and our society, and for levering ourselves and our world into a happier reality? But if history were presented as a lever for change, not as a shrine for old myths, would its present supporters allow it space in the curriculum?

The author of chapter 3, Timothy J. Stanley, explores some of the less palatable manifestations of historical consciousness, public memory, and history education in Canadian history. Public memory in Canada, he argues, has worked effectively to erase racism from historical consciousness. Pervasive racism does not square with accounts that describe the national past as an inevitable progress towards Canada's status as 'the best country in the world.' His essay examines some of the common myths about racism in Canada and its links to forms of historical memory. Specifically, he examines a nationalist grand narrative that seems unable to represent on-going racist practices and their consequences, including the daily realities of physical and psychic brutality experienced by many and the consistent privilege experienced by others. Particular ways of representing the past, he maintains, do not just condone but *contribute* to exclusions in the present. Finally, Stanley considers alternative, potentially more inclusive, ways of imagining the past as part of a broad strategy for anti-racism and historical education.

In chapter 4 Keith Barton draws on his extensive research in the field of history education, including his research into how children in Northern Ireland and the United States think about the past. Barton explores the potential for history education to contribute to citizenship in pluralist, participatory democracies, a potential that, he argues, provides the only justification for including history education within a publicly funded school system. Debates over public memory often revolve around narrow interpretations of what constitutes 'real' history, with each side attempting to establish its own approach as authoritative and dismissing all rivals. Barton, by contrast, examines the multiple historical 'acts' – such as analysis, identification, and the exercise of moral judgment – that students are expected to perform in school, and the ways in which these reflect the varied, and frequently conflicting, public uses of history. He argues that history education should not be evaluated by its adherence to an exclusive (and supposedly authoritative) body of content, skills, or procedures, but by its contribution to democratic citizenship – a contribution that can best be achieved through a focus on the purposes and practices of humanistic education.

Like Barton, the next essayist, Jocelyn Létourneau, draws on his research into what young people think about the past. A frequent complaint by social commentators, historians, and educators is that young people know very little about history, and when students are asked focused, specific questions about Canadian history, this seems to be true. But when the same students are asked to account for the historical experience of the group to which they feel they belong – Québécois, for example – Létourneau finds that their knowledge of the past is much more fluent and abundant. Students have a coherent and, indeed, fixed understanding of 'what really happened.' Their historical knowledge, however, does not seem to be influenced primarily by the work of professional historians or the texts and lessons of their history class-rooms. Létourneau's essay asks the disturbing question of whether it is possible, with the traditional sources of historical knowledge used in schools (teaching, readers, manuals, etc.), to influence and reorient students' vision of the past – to teach them something different from what they *already believe* about history – while their collective memory (which is contradicted on many points of 'fact' by the work of professional historians) exerts such a strong influence in shaping their historical consciousness.

In the next essay, Chad Gaffield argues that historians in Canada have, over the past forty years, participated in some remarkable changes in the way they teach, write about, and give meaning to Canadian history. This blossoming of Canadian historical scholarship that began in the 1960s occurred during a period when history education was the object of intense debate at all levels of schooling. One unfortunate result was that new Canadian research did not easily find its way into the history curriculum, to begin the revision of public memory. Gaffield argues that a new approach to Canadian history education now integrates the ambition of research intensiveness (usually identified with professional historians) with the potential of active learning (usually identified with progressive teaching practices) in both schools and universities. An approach to teaching history that is based on the use of primary sources promises to move forward debate about educational policy and content, and, Gaffield argues, to influence our individual and collective understandings of Canada's past.

The final essay in the book is, as I noted above, a remarkable reflection by Ken Osborne, the venerated teacher, history educator, and historian of education at the University of Manitoba. He provides not only a thoughtful overview and synthesis of the issues raised in the six preceding essays, but an overview and synthesis of the important issues in history education in Canada past, present, and future.

The reflections – I hesitate to say solutions – provided in this volume on the 'problem' of history education in Canada are varied. One major theme not touched on by these (male) authors is the issue of gender – does gender influence historical consciousness, and, if so, how? I leave this key question to another volume. The contributors to this book write about a variety of issues and themes, but they are united in their articulation of two broad themes. All question, to some extent, the ways that history is being taught in Canada. On any level, a subject that is routinely known as the 'most boring' in school has lots of room for improvement. But the authors also raise the possibility that the ways in which history is generally taught – as a fixed body of known 'facts' – may be linked to some of the deeper problems that we, as a society, have about how knowledge, identity, and power are created and sustained within our social system. If history were taught in a more culturally sensitive, critical, interactive, and disciplined way, would Canadians be better prepared to take a more active role in the kinds of citizenship needed for the coming century? Would they be more willing to do so? You will make up your own minds as you read these thought-provoking essays.

1 What Is Historical Consciousness?

PETER SEIXAS

The three terms that are used to frame the essays in this collection – public memory, citizenship, and history education – are tremendously rich. I want to start with an exploration of their meanings.

Public Memory

What does the term 'public memory' mean, and how is it different from history? Both history and memory have to do with our understanding of the past, but there is a difference in their connotations. 'History' invokes notions of objectivity and science. 'Memory' invokes notions of subjectivity and feeling. 'History' has a method. 'Memory,' if it is there at all, is immediately so. Consider such popular usages as 'Remembrance Day.' This is about an uncritical and immediate connection with the past, and it is full of feeling. Or the license plate 'Je me souviens.' This is about a powerful link between a group in the present and events of a quarter of a millennium ago. Think for a moment about how well Remembrance Day would work as History Day. Not very. Or perhaps a licence plate with the slogan 'Je connais l'histoire.'

Adding the term 'public' to 'memory' gives us something more. Public, or collective, memory retains the immediacy of individual memory, but it also depends on what French historian Pierre Nora has called 'lieux de memoire,' or sites of memory. Our common, collective, or public, memory is built and maintained through a range of structures, symbols, and practices: statues, commemorations, place names, symbols, films. Without these structural supports, memory of a particular event or person fades from the public consciousness. Literary critic Kerwin Klein calls the phenomenon 'structural memory.' (And, for reasons I won't go into, public or collective memory has become an explosive field of study in the past twenty years.)

Public memory is important, because it is not just about the past, which is, after all, finished. Public memory brings the past into present consciousness and allows it to be mobilized for decisions about the future. (After September 11, we saw this in references to Pearl Harbor as well as Vietnam, mobilizing two very different kinds of trajectories for responses in the present.) The Orwellian commonplace applies here: 'who controls the past controls the future.' And that is why there are furious debates about public memory.

Citizenship

The second term, citizenship, in its commonsense usage, has to do with the relationship of individuals to the group: their rights and responsibilities. But not just any group can be a partner in the relationship of citizenship: citizenship is the relationship specifically of the individual to the modern state, which has the legitimate power to exercise the collective will of its members.

I have colleagues who want to define citizenship much more broadly, a theme that Keith Barton takes up in chapter 4. They think it would be a good thing to teach young people that they are citizens of the world, in order to promote global responsibility. But I argue that in the absence of a world government or state, which can enforce the collective will of citizens, using the term 'citizenship' in this context is more a hopeful metaphor than a reflection of reality.

The exercise of collective will depends to a certain extent upon a common public sense of where the collective has been and where it should go – a loose narrative trajectory that situates decisions in the present between an imagined past and an imagined future. This is one of the important links between public memory and citizenship.

Now, a sense of that narrative trajectory, which has always been difficult in multinational states like Canada, has become even more complex in current cultural conditions. Our notion of citizenship has to take these conditions into consideration. These are the complicating features that I would highlight:

- transnational migration (visible change in neighbourhoods, schools, workplaces within one decade)
- globalization (economic interpenetration and dependencies)
- technological development (even where we are not physically living

next to people with different senses of trajectories, peoples of the
world are exposed to each others' ideas virtually)
- radical political rearrangements (fall of the Soviet regime and
changes in Latin America, eastern Europe, South Africa)
- empowerment of previously disempowered groups (e.g., women,
ethnic minorities) even where regimes have not toppled
- deflation of forward-looking projects of the nation-state and
socialism

These features can be summed up in Chinua Achebe's phrase 'things
fall apart' and characterized as the condition of both modernity and
postmodernity.

History Education

We can now begin to define the third term, history education, in ways
that build on the above definitions of public memory and citizenship.
From the beginnings of mass public schooling in the nineteenth century,
history education was seen as a place to construct public memory and
thereby to construct the nation. And many people today continue to see
it in this way. History textbooks, school observances of Remembrance
Days, the daily instructional practices of social studies teachers can all be
interpreted as Nora's *lieux de memoires*. If this were to be the role of history
teaching in the schools, then debates about school curriculum would be
framed around the question 'What public memory *should we teach?'*
Essentially, which stories about the past should our students learn?

This set of questions would separate what goes on in school history
from the construction of public memory that takes place in much of
popular culture, in movies like (for example) *We Were Soldiers*, *Dances
with Wolves*, or *Independence Day*, and in television, historical fiction,
music, and video games. These media are not subject to direct public
policy deliberations in the way that curriculum decisions are. But I am
going to make the argument that schools and universities have a *special*
role, that goes beyond the shaping of public memory. We *need* something more than that in the cultural conditions I described earlier.

One response to the sense that things are falling apart involves the
attempt to reconstruct what seems to have been lost: an authentic
history grounded in a cohesive community. In the United States, Chester
Finn, Arthur Schlesinger, Jr, Lynn Cheney, and others have spent more
than a decade trying to shore up, at least for the public, a form of history
that seemed like a lost cause in academe – that is, the coherent narrative

of the progress of the nation. In Canada, some of those who were most responsible for getting history education back into the public debate have had a similar agenda. There have been explicit links among the campaign for more standardized Canadian history in the schools, the celebration of political heroes, and the promotion of the politics of Canadian national unity and identity.

For example, the cause of public memory in Canada has been well served by the impeccably timed and well-publicized Dominion Institute surveys. Here are some questions from the quiz whose results were published in July 2001:

1. Who was the first prime minister of Canada?
5. In 1944, Canadians joined in an event called D-Day. What happened on that day?
9. What year did Confederation occur?

If the aim is to get a broad Canadian public talking about the importance of history, then these surveys are the unrivalled leaders, and the Dominion Institute has thus performed a most valuable task. But the danger is that this kind of survey sends history education policy in a certain direction, a direction that I will argue is problematic and inadequate. It is not at all clear that a resurrected, monumental narrative, the construction of a simple public memory, can meet the felt needs for a usable past that will help orient young people for the future – that is, to help them as citizens – in the complex, rapidly changing, and conflict-ridden world they face.

We need to set higher standards than this. When I say 'higher standards,' I do not simply mean that students need to know more facts, or get more of them right. Rather, we need to acknowledge that contention over the meanings of the past is an ongoing feature of contemporary culture, and that it might even be constructive, if citizens had ways to participate knowledgeably and thoughtfully. This conception of public participation in the critical interpretation of the past requires quite a different vision of history education, one that is required by the demands of contemporary citizenship to go beyond the inculcation of public memory.

Historical Consciousness

When I agreed to participate in the lecture series and the publication of this collection of essays, I promised that I would explore the question of what is 'historical consciousness.' At this point, I cannot imagine a better definition, than the intersection among public memory, citizenship, and history education. But another way to come at historical consciousness is through a series of questions.

These questions are asked by everyone, from elementary school children, to politicians, to historians.

1. How did things get to be as we see them today? Which aspects are signs of continuity over time, and which are signs of change? These questions are not morally neutral or disinterested. They ask for accounts of the past to explain the present, and their answers have implications for the future. So, is the Taliban's interpretation of Islam something new, or is it rooted in an ongoing tradition?
2. What group or groups am I a part of, and what are its/their origins? In fact, my identity has various aspects that take me to various different points of origin.
3. How should we judge each other's past actions? By extension, what debts does my group owe to others and/or others to mine? These questions encompass reparations, land claims, restitutions, and apologies. The BC government's referendum on land claims merely gives new shape to the question of who owes what to whom in a way that rests fundamentally on historical interpretations.
4. Are things basically getting better or are they getting worse? This is the question of progress and decline. In 1993 Robert Heilbroner asked whether the worst was yet to come. We asked the same question on September 11, and again when Ariel Sharon sent tanks into the West Bank.
5. What stories about the past should I believe? On what grounds? Oliver Stone's account in *JFK*? Daniel Goldhagen's explanation of the Holocaust? Marc Starowicz's history of Canada? These questions raise the problem of evidence.
6. Which stories shall we tell? What about the past is significant enough to pass on to others, and particularly to the next generation?
7. Is there anything we can do to make things better? Can I – we – do any thing more to stop global warming than not buying a Lincoln Navigator SUV?

Let me highlight three characteristics of these questions:

• They are not just about the past: they form a link between past, present, and future.

- They are naturally occurring questions in our culture today. They are not just historians' questions: they are everybody's.
- At the same time, precisely because of the cultural conditions I outlined earlier, though they are natural to ask, they are more difficult to answer.

Helping young people formulate good answers to these questions of historical consciousness is, I would argue, the central task of history education. But what *are* good answers? Let's explore this through an exercise with a primary source, an excerpt from a speech by John A. Macdonald on 4 May 1885:

> The Chinese are foreigners. If they come to this country, after three years' residence, they may, if they choose, be naturalized. But still we know that when the Chinaman comes here he intends to return to his own country; he does not bring his family with him; he is a stranger, a sojourner in a strange land, for his own purposes for a while; he has no common interest with us, and while he gives us his labor and is paid for it, and is valuable, the same as a threshing machine or any other agricultural implement which we may borrow from the United States on hire and return it to the owner on the south side of the line; a Chinaman gives us his labor and gets his money, but that money does not fructify in Canada; he does not invest it here, but takes it with him and returns to China; and if he cannot, his executors or his friends send his body back to the flowery land. But he has no British instincts or British feelings or aspirations, and therefore ought not to have a vote.[1]

Think back to some of the questions of historical consciousness, and consider how they can draw a relationship between us as citizens in Canada in 2002 and the text from 1885:

- Do we see continuity here or change?
- What does this statement from a 'father of Confederation' tell us about our origins? Our collective identity?
- Are things getting better or are they getting worse?

In thinking about students' answers to these questions, I would start to define what makes a good answer with criteria like the following:

1. Comprehending the interpretive choices and constraints involved in using traces from the past to construct historical accounts.

2. Understanding the *pastness* of the past, the distance between the present and the past, and the difficulty in representing the past in the present. At the same time (paradoxically), understanding the presence of the past – that is, the consequences for us today of earlier actions and decisions.
3. Acknowledging complexity and uncertainty; dealing with multiple causes, conflicting belief systems, and historical actors' differing perspectives.

Helping students to be able to respond in these ways suggests a considerably more challenging history education agenda than that implied by the Dominion Institute surveys. More challenging but more relevant.

Theoretical contributions from British history education research can help to take this project forward. One key is the notion of *second order historical concepts*. Peter Lee and Ros Ashby explain that second order concepts 'are not what history is "about," but they shape the way we go about doing history.'[2] They also call them 'procedural' concepts. Three central second order concepts in the British work are evidence, accounts, and cause. Neither young people nor historians necessarily articulate definitions for these concepts, but they have to use them in knowing or explaining the past. Unlike the answer to the question about who was the first prime minister of Canada, how to use the concept of historical 'cause' or 'evidence' is not something that a student either *knows* or *does not know*. Rather, the British look for what they call *progression* in understanding of these concepts. Space limitations allow me to give you only the briefest sense of the investigation into children's ideas about the second order concept of historical accounts.

Lee and Ashby gave elementary school students two cartoon-strip stories about the Roman conquest of the Britons, divided into three 'chapters' each. The two stories present two very different interpretations. The first story begins 'Before the Romans came the Britons lived in wooden huts. They had no towns. Almost no-one could read. The Britons often fought one another.' In the next episode, 'The Romans went to Britain and took most of it over. They made Britain peaceful.' The other story begins quite differently: 'Before the Romans came the Britons had their own way of life. They were good at making jewellery and tools ...' In chapter 2: 'The Romans took Britain over. They beat the Britons who tried to stop them.' Examining students' answers, Lee and Ashby were interested in knowing how students explained the fact that there were two different accounts of the same set of events.

They got responses like the following: 'You don't know, we wasn't there when it happened. It might have been passed down but it could have been changed or forgotten.'[3] They developed a hierarchy of sophistication in handling this problem – the very basic problem of handling conflicting accounts, which tells us something about how children understand the relationship between the account of the past and the past itself. This hierarchy is the beginning of a map of progression in young people's concepts of accounts.

Progression in students' ideas about accounts and their relation to the past are provided here, adapted from Lee and Ashby's list:[4]

- The past is inaccessible. We can't know – we weren't there.
- Available information determines the accounts about the past. Differences in accounts are a result of gaps of information and mistakes.
- The past is reported in a more or less biased way. Differences in accounts are a result of distortion (in the form of lies, exaggeration, dogmatism). The problem is not just a lack of information (the focus shifts to the author).
- Stories are written (perhaps necessarily) from a legitimate position held by the author. Differences in accounts are a result of selection.

Largely as a result of the British research, the British National Curriculum, unlike any current North American curriculum, has been explicitly built on the second order concepts as learning outcomes. Using questions of historical consciousness, I have developed a larger list of second order concepts. By building on the British work, these can provide the framework for a different kind of history education. These concepts include:

- evidence
- significance
- continuity and change
- progress and decline
- empathy/perspective taking
- moral judgment
- agency

Let me point out one example of how this is different from the British work: you see that 'cause' is not on my list. It has been replaced by 'agency.' Notions of 'agency' structure our sense of how possible it is for particular people or particular groups to shape and reshape the course of events in history, as they come up against the structural constraints that have been handed down from the past. Although it is very closely related to the notion of 'cause,' it brings forward the questions of differential power that have been at the centre of recent historiography. Moreover, it raises questions about students' understanding of their own place in history, their own sense of themselves as historical agents (thus as citizens).

Once again, second order concepts underlie all of our attempts at coming to terms with the past and its implications for decisions in the present. They are not 'all or nothing': students can get better at understanding them, using them, and working with them. History education should be aimed at helping them to do so.

Reconstructing history curriculum using second order concepts will not be easy. I want to present a small picture of the challenge and the promise. In a study of students' understanding of 'significance' that I conducted a number of years ago, I asked approximately eighty-five students in four Grade 11 social studies classrooms to sketch a diagram of the most significant events, trends, and people in all of world history, to arrange them on the page in a way that made sense, and to give an explanation of why they had written what they did. They had about five minutes to make the sketch.

If you know that the British Columbia social studies curriculum deals with twentieth century Canadian history in Grade 11, the response of Walt, the first student, will be understandable to you. On the left, he has a bubble that says 'the great depression, more women and children than men work.' This is linked to 'Canadians,' 'conscription brought in,' 'Men chose to go to war,' 'Help in World War I,' 'Vimy Ridge, Ypres, Passchendale,' and finally, 'Help in World War II.' Walt selected a series of discrete items. He said he put these down because they were what he remembered. His logic was this, basically: if these were *not* the most significant events, why were the teacher and textbook focusing on them?

Tom's response is different:

Stone Age
Become industrial
Wars
Inventions of cars, planes
Very awful story in general

Computers invented
Technology boom
Virtual reality
Cd rom
Not many wars at all

Tom was perhaps paying less attention in class, or at least he did not use the information from the current school year to define his sense of historical significance. What he has done, however, is to assemble the beginning of a narrative account (and remember, this was not part of the task as I had defined it). We see a concern with technology, and some notion of progress, from 'very awful story' to 'not many wars at all' and perhaps some implicit notions of moral judgment and agency.

Finally, Yvonne included the following:

World is created
Rise of homo sapiens
Factories are built
Cars are invented
The rise of convenience
Plastic is invented
More convenience
CFC's are invented
Convenience and comfort
World is slowly destroyed

This sketch has a fully developed narrative trajectory, from the past to the present and future, embedded with concerns of agency, and moral judgment, expressed with an almost poetic irony. This response taught me something about historical significance: that the significance of a particular event – such as the invention of CFCs – is entirely dependent upon the larger narrative of which it is a part.

Conclusion

What do young people need to learn in order to make sense of their place in time – in this place, in these times – and what can we do to help them? Perhaps in the past, it was enough to hand down an engaging story of origins and heroes. Though the transmission of this kind of narrative may serve some purpose at some stage of history education, it is not enough for a multinational, multicultural, and globalizing society. There are too many origins, too many heroes, too many stories. We cannot escape the knowledge that there are different, but legitimate, ways to put them together, that convey very different messages about who we are, where we have been, and where we might be headed. Choosing only one to believe and convey would be a deliberate blinding.

What is needed in history education can be glimpsed in part from the processes and habits of mind of historians. Their starting points are open and flexible frameworks for understanding the past, not polished and finished stories. They read the documentary traces of the past, using them to construct larger narratives and arguments about what happened and what it means. They fit small, individual pieces, insignificant in themselves, into larger contexts and then rethink the meanings of the larger pictures. They confront questions of agency: how individuals and groups have confronted the opportunities and constraints inherited from their pasts. They read and listen to, and then criticize and argue with, each other. They challenge each other's interpretations, on the basis of sources and their uses. They understand their narratives as arguments, and thus as tentative contributions to an ongoing conversation. The challenge for history education is to devise ways to introduce young people to these same historical tools, processes, and ways of thinking, not in order to make them mini-historians, or to give them an early start on academic careers; rather, to help them make sense of who they are, where they stand, and what they can do – as individuals, as members of multiple, intersecting groups, and as citizens with roles and responsibilities in relation to nations and states in a complex, conflict-ridden, and rapidly changing world.

In a time when identities are experienced as fluid and overlapping, when debates rage over the redress of historical wrongs, when the democratic state is challenged from inside and out, it is not enough to discharge responsibilities for history education by developing a mythic public memory that feels good, even if the funding can be generated to replicate Hollywood production values in the newest of new media. The waters are too troubled.

In order to have a usable history, young people have to be able to understand the meanings of the past for their lives in the present. But without notions of evidence, without the ability to assess contending interpretations, without a sense of the choices, both moral and epistemological, that go into constructing a historical narrative, they will not have the tools they need to take part in the ongoing discussions of the meanings of the past that are essential to building community in a fractured, dynamic, and rapidly changing set of cultural circumstances.

NOTES

1 Canada, House of Commons, *Debates*, 4 May 1885, p. 1582.
2 P. Lee and R. Ashby, 'Progression in Historical Understanding in Students Ages 7–14,' in P. Stearns, P. Seixas, and S. Wineburg, eds., *Knowing, Teaching, and Learning History: National and International Perspectives* (New York: New York University Press, 2000).
3 Ibid., 206.
4 Ibid., 212.

2 Canadian History Teaching in Canada: What's the Big Deal?

DESMOND MORTON

'The past is a foreign country,' wrote an otherwise obscure English novelist, L.P. Hartley. 'They do things differently there.'[1] An American scholar, David Lowenthal, borrowed the phrase for a book that distinguishes between history and heritage. History, he suggests, is the past; heritage is what we make of it.[2] You see the difference at L'Anse aux Meadows in Newfoundland, at Old Fort Henry, or in the Secondary 4th History Exam in Quebec. We start with a concern for the past; we finish preoccupied by a concern for politically correct interpretation, for attracting paying visitors, for ensuring that values and concepts approved by ministries, boards, and editors have been memorized by the young.

The past does not change, but its interpretation can alter radically. In Quebec, Jocelyn Létourneau has offended nationalists by arguing that their cause has largely been successful.[3] As his essay in this collection will suggest, Confederation, with its deep diversity, has worked. French is stronger. There is, in contemporary Canada, both 'sovereignty' and 'association.' More radically, Gérard Bouchard's proposed 'Américanicité' invites us to trace our roots from America's first people, as is common in Mexico or Peru, rather than from European ancestors.[4] This does not change history, but it certainly alters the perspective and the 'us.' Both Bouchard and Létourneau use history as a feedstock for challenging heritage. Both use the past to interpret the present, for reasons that are not hard to understand. And neither approach is utterly new. Marius Barbeau, T.F. McIlwraith, and other Canadian ethnologists in the 1930s antedated Bouchard's arguments, and George Brown, George Stanley, and other English-speaking historians denounced the doom-laden teaching of Lionel Groulx's disciples in the so-called Montreal School. History is perennially 'new' and also faithfully old.

'We Haven't a Clue'

Back in 1997, the Donner Foundation financed the young Dominion Institute to hire pollsters from Angus Reid to ask more or less the same kind of questions of 1,024 Canadians, aged eighteen to twenty-four. The results, announced on Canada Day, were more or less what reporters usually discovered when the city editor sent them up to the campus on a quiet day in the newsroom. Most Canadians had no idea when Confederation happened. One-third could not even place it in the right century. Most (63 per cent) knew that Macdonald was our first prime minister, though in Quebec awareness of that fact dropped to 28 per cent. *En revanche*, 79 per cent of Quebeckers but only 33 per cent of New Brunswickers knew that Wilfrid Laurier was our first francophone prime minister. Two out of five in the sample imagined that Canada had fought France, Britain, and Russia during the two world wars.[5] No one could define 'responsible government.' No one dared ask the question.

Later that year, on the fiftieth anniversary of Citizenship Day, 1947, the institute announced that 45 per cent of 1,350 Canadians had flunked a standardized twelve-question citizenship test. Respondents could not name all three of the oceans that border Canada nor the event that brought the original provinces together. Most thought that Canada's head of state is the prime minister. (Come to think of it, so did Brian Mulroney.) And the tests kept coming. A Remembrance Day quiz revealed that some Canadians believed *we* attacked Pearl Harbor. Some kind of wish-fulfilment, perhaps! In ensuing years, Canadians got used to a twice-yearly institute reminder that 'we haven't a clue' about ourselves.

Canadian ignorance of our history is a commonplace, and not just among professors. Politicians and business leaders repeat the mantra. My friend and sometimes co-author, Jack Granatstein, won best-seller status for a little book claiming that Canadian history had been killed, mainly by academic social historians and educational bureaucrats, though, as cultural commentator Robert Fulford pointed out, no one is entirely free of blame – except Jack.[6]

None of this, incidentally, is new – or unique to Canada. In the 1980s, Reagan sympathizers found a similar lamentable ignorance among Americans. Two-thirds of them couldn't date the Civil War; one-third put it in the wrong century. British studies in the Thatcher era found similar bad news. The difference is that people in Canada started to do something about it. Canada's National History Society, the people who publish the *Beaver* in Winnipeg, persuaded Rideau Hall to issue a Governor General's Award to outstanding school history teachers. Charles R. Bronfman's CRB Foundation worked for years on 'Heritage Minutes' and other ways to inform Canadians about their history. In 1999, the Bronfman-funded McGill Institute for the Study of Canada held a national conference called grandly L'avenir du passé/ Giving Our Past a Future. By coincidence, the former CEO of Bell Canada, Linton 'Red' Wilson, had pledged half a million dollars of his own money to revive history in Canada – perhaps using new technologies in which his firm was expert. That led to a merger with the CRB resources and an organization called Historica.

Was History Dead?

To be fair, though Jack Granatstein is a friend, I never believed that Canada's history was dead. I grant that it lacks the bloodshed and myth making of some histories, but I think that mass murder is shameful and myths are often nonsense. I knew from experience that history was hard to teach, but rejoiced that there were some very fine and successful teachers to emulate, most of them in Canadian high schools. And Quebec's minister of education, Pauline Marois, promised that she would teach her sons to cook, if only their schools taught them about the past.[7]

People kept telling us that Canada's history is worth knowing, even sometimes fun. When Canadians curl up with a good non-fiction book, chances are fifty-fifty that it will be about history. Huge audiences stayed glued to televised versions of the U.S. Civil War and to histories of baseball and jazz. A history channel was such a success with U.S. audiences that the CRTC gave quick approval to Canada's History Channel, and then to a Canal d'histoire. For more than $25 million, the CBC and Radio Canada staged *Canada: A People's History*, its most popular series in years.

Dreaming About the Past?

So why the gloom? One common thread linked Reagan, Thatcher, and the Donner Foundation. All were, in contemporary terms, conservatives, and a conservative is often someone who thinks the past is preferable to the present and probably to the future. This is an interesting but utopian position, as the past is a place we can never really revisit, however we try, any more than we can predict the future. Conservatives need the past as a guidepost. Would Canada be falling apart if Canadians understood their history? Would Québécois have voted No if they remembered all those cruel episodes of victimization? Would Canadians be as alienated from their political system as they seem to be if they – and perhaps current practitioners – understood the rules and how to make them express legitimate concerns?

History, said Henry Ford, 'is more or less bunk.'[8] In the sense he had learned it, he was probably right. Whatever Ford meant, postmodernists know that there is no single 'true' history, only many personal versions, some of which are chosen by education officials and 'approved for childish consumption.' The Dominion Institute's solution to the ignorance it discovered was to be a collection of free-floating 'National Standards,' purged of any troubling or debatable context. But is knowing that Confederation happened in 1867 or the Winnipeg General Strike in 1919 'history' or simply an almost meaningless fragment of an event, a 'factoid' as easily forgotten as memorized?

A History of History?

Ironically, in a debate about history, there seems to be little awareness of the history of teaching history. Public education was a nineteenth-century invention, designed to create loyal, dutiful citizens, and history was its sharpest blade. Properly trained young men would be patriotic conscripts in the ranks of national armies, and patriotic women would cheer their son's departure to the latest national war. No wonder provinces have watched over this aspect of education with a special passion. Years ago, when I agreed to write a book for British Columbia's Grade 11 program, a colleague reminded me of a predecessor. As headmaster of Upper Canada College and a decorated veteran who had left a leg in France, W.L. Grant must have seemed an ideal man to write British Columbia's first Canadian history text. But when he dared to explain why Quebeckers had refused to support Conscription in 1917, his book was promptly scrapped.[9] As I adjusted to historical pronouncements from Victoria, Grant came often to mind.

Heritage making may explain why approved versions of our history have, in Maurice Hutton's phrase, been as 'dull as ditchwater.'[10] As a member of the famous Massey-Lévesque Commission on Canada's culture, Professor Hilda Neatby reserved special venom for school history.[11] In 1962, Northrop Frye told the Toronto School Board that not much would be lost 'if history, as presently prescribed and taught, were dropped entirely from the curriculum.'[12] A decade later, in *What Culture? What Heritage?*, Bernard Hodgetts published a savage denunciation of how young Canadians were taught their history. Professor Ken Osborne, a veteran of the history and social studies scene, concluded in 1996: 'It seems reasonably clear that most students are not being led to think about the Canadian past ... in any coherent or systematic way.'[13] And Osborne added that he knew of no 'golden age' for Canadian history teachers or learners.

Translated, revised, purified, and modernized, school history is obliged to pay homage to current adult orthodoxy, be it British imperialism, papal authority, Marxism, bilingual multiculturalism, feminism, or the George W. Bush world view. This is not new. Confederation happened at a time in western civilization when school-based history had provided the core of civic education for future members of a mass electorate. By assigning education to the provinces, the authors of Confederation ensured that there would be no pan-Canadian orthodoxy. Jack Granatstein wants a unifying national history. Could Canada survive the 'History Wars' other countries have experienced?

Historical Thinking

As pain-averse professionals, most official educators outside Quebec have preferred to diminish history to the smallest possible compass. Postmodern doubts about the 'accuracy' of history have accelerated their urge. Much that makes history fascinating and perhaps even educational tends to outrage an authoritarian. If history is not true, how dare you teach it to the young? The answer, of course, is to invite close study of the same rules of evidence and human behaviour that a citizen should learn to apply to commercial advertising, political speeches, and ministry circulars. End of argument!

Through the study of history, students could learn 'historical understanding': the fundamentals of causation, sequence, and relationships that distinguish 'history' in its full intellectual rigor from that magpie's nest of diamonds and baubles called 'heritage.' Such an approach, as Quebec's leading popular historian, Jacques Lacoursière, argued in his 1997 report to the provincial government, is rich in the 'skills' that preoccupy contemporary educational policymakers. In the report of his working group, Lacoursière summarized the benefits of teaching 'historical thinking':

> It is through history that we understand the mechanisms of change and continuity, and the many ways in which problems are posed and resolved in society. We learn to recognize and weigh the different interests beliefs, experiences and circumstances that guide human beings inside and outside their own societies, in the past and in the present. History enables us to understand how such interests, beliefs and experiences drive human beings to construct knowledge, and makes us aware of the value of knowledge and of its relative nature.[14]

What Can We Learn?

In history, as in much else, much more is taught than is learned. Assuming we had the power to inspire learning, what would we seek from history?

1. *Appreciation of the continuum of past, present, and future.* Almost nothing is totally without precedent, though the circumstances will be only imperfectly recalled. That imperfection, aggravated by the subjectivity of time, space, and circumstance, is as important to teach as whatever purports to be an interpretation of the past. Time-past, time-present is a philosophical concept, by no means self-evident to the very young, any more than that other historical concept, cause and effect. Yet it lies at the core of civic reasoning.
2. *Awareness of cultural, ethnic, and family heritage.* Canadians are not members of a rootless society. People have lived here for at least twenty millennia, and we or our ancestors have come here from somewhere else, bringing experiences and culture with us. Canadians need to recognize the common experiences that form their culture and they need a sense of the heritages with which we share our country. We need to know about minorities and about majorities too. History provides the means.
3. *Understanding how and why our society has evolved.* We need a kind of 'user's manual' understanding of Canada, our province, and our community. We should know how the workings have changed over time, sometimes by external pressure, sometimes because individuals no greater than ourselves have pressed for change. This is some-

times described as 'civics,' but history is not limited to the framework of democratic institutions and government. History extends to business, industry, financial institutions, unions, and the multiple organizations of civil society.

4. *Knowledge of our world.* However unsatisfying the state of Canadian history may be, world history has virtually disappeared from school curricula save as seldom-taught electives. Yet we live in an interconnected world. The ancestral roots of our own people, communications media, and our own economic past, present, and future, make Canadians part of that world. If ignorance of our own country is disturbing, ignorance of the world is dangerous. Because we lack any sense of world history, our collective responses to the world are frequently child-like. Contemporary history will provide you with examples.

Learning from Uncertainty

Having defined some of the benefits we expect from a greater understanding of history, we must ask how close we are to these goals. Can we come closer? Can we persuade teachers, students, and, above all, their elected and appointed bosses, of the value of 'historical understanding'? Can we convince Canadians to broaden their array of historical perceptions? Can we make better use of existing and potential media and resources? Any exploration of the problems of learning, understanding, and sharing history, such as happens annually at Historica's teachers' institutes, reveals hundreds of good ideas, some of them contradictory, some mutually reinforcing, all of them worth sharing.

The obvious complications of mobilizing nationwide interest in a diverse set of provincial curricula could be met by a national organization of Canadian history teachers, sharing experience and techniques, developing resources, and expanding the interprovincial consortia that have emerged in both western and Atlantic Canada. A national association could also support and encourage professionalism among history teachers, who otherwise are among the most exposed and vulnerable members of their profession.

History in Canada seems to me to be very much alive. It is also full of challenging uncertainties and fresh ideas. It is grabbing a larger market than the readership of academic monographs. Between the CBC, Historica, the History Channel, the *Beaver*, and countless local, provincial, and federal initiatives, it is passing through a vigorous era. A national history teachers organization could consolidate some of the gains.

NOTES

1 See L.P. Hartley, *The Go-Between* (London: Hamish-Hamilton, 1953), 1.
2 David Lowenthal, *The Past Is a Foreign Country* (Cambridge: Cambridge University Press, 1985), xvi. Lowenthal pursued the distinction between history and heritage in *Possessed by the Past: The Heritage Crusade and the Spoils of History* (New York: Cambridge University, Press, 1966).
3 Jocelyn Létourneau, *Passer à l'avenir: histoire, mémoire, identité dans le Québec d'aujourd'hui* (Montreal: Les Éditions Boréal, 2000), 'Québec/Canada sondage: les frères siamois,' *L'Actualité*, 1 November 1998, 27–36, and 'C'est la faute à l'histoire,' ibid., 38–40.
4 On *Américanité*, see Gérard Bouchard, *Genèse des nations et cultures du Nouveau Monde* (Montreal: Les Éditions Boréal, 2001), esp. 12–17.
5 *Globe and Mail*, 1 July 1997. On the Dominion Institute, see Daniel Gardner et al., *Youth and History: A Policy Paper for the Dominion Institute of Toronto* (Toronto: Dominion Institute, 1997), 8–10.
6 J.L. Granatstein, *Who Killed Canadian History?* (Toronto: HarperCollins, 1998). For criticism, see, J.R. Miller, 'The Invisible Historian,' *Journal of the Canadian Historical Association* (1997): 3–18.
7 See Louise Gendron, 'École: Maman le ministre,' *L'Actualité*, 15 September 1997, 16–21.
8 As cited by A. Norman Jaffares and Martin Gray, *The Collins Dictionary of Quotations* (Glasgow: Collins, 1995), 261 as found in the *Chicago Tribune*, 1916.
9 On W.L. Grant as author of a B.C. history, see Charles Humphries, 'The Banning of a Book in British Columbia,' *B.C. Studies* 1, no. 1 (1968–9): 1–12.
10 Cited by F.H. Underhill in the *Canadian Historical Review* 16 (1935): 336.
11 See Hilda Neatby, 'National History,' in *Studies for the Royal Commission on Arts and Letters in Canada* (Ottawa: King's Printer, 1951). The problems of defining a 'national' history for Canada were reviewed by Marcel Trudel and Geneviève Jain for the Royal Commission on Bilingualism and Biculturalism. See 'Canadian History Textbooks: A Comparative Study,' in *Studies for the Royal Commission on Bilingualism and Biculturalism* (Ottawa: Queen's Printer, 1970).
12 Northrop Frye, *Design for Learning* (Toronto: University of Toronto Press,

1962). A better-known blast at the state of history teaching was Bernard Hodgets, *What Culture? What Heritage?* (Toronto: Ontario Institute for Studies in Education, 1972).

13 Ken Osborne, 'Teaching Heritage in the Classroom' (unpublished paper), 165, 171.

14 Jacques Lacoursière et al., *Learning from the Past: Report of the Task Force on the Teaching of History* (Quebec, 10 May 1996), 3.

3 Whose Public? Whose Memory? Racisms, Grand Narratives, and Canadian History

TIMOTHY J. STANLEY

The myth that there is no racism in Canada endures. Many people living in Canada confidently assume that racism either exists elsewhere (in the United States, for example) or that, if it does exist in this country, it is an unfortunate exception to otherwise civilized and tolerant norms. Yet, as thousands of Canadians are only too well aware, racism is alive and well in Canada. Far from being exceptional, it is an ever-present reality, part of their daily lives.

For many Canadians, racism is an individual moral failing. The idea of widespread racist exclusion simply does not square with what they see as 'the best country in the world.' Canada, after all, is not the former Yugoslavia or apartheid South Africa or the United States under Jim Crow. Thus, Canadians' descriptions of racist experiences often appear unbelievable and are denied – explained away as either the results of unfortunate misunderstandings or the product of over-fertile imaginations and questionable motives on the part of those describing such experiences. But such experiences of racism are not just reflections of individual prejudices. They are systematic practices, institutional patterns of exclusion, and taken-for-granted systems of representation. They are as much cultural as they are individual. They shape the meanings that we encounter as we navigate our everyday worlds and determine whose meanings we take seriously and engage critically, and whose we ignore and dismiss. In this context, people's accounts of experiences of racism in Canada are more often than not true.

Public memory is one of the ways through which racist exclusion is effected. By selectively representing the histories of the many people who live in Canada, by identifying certain people as Canadian and largely ignoring the others, and by sanitizing the histories through which some people have become dominant, public memory sets the stage for racist denial. Meanwhile, the relative silence of public memory on the racism that has helped to create Canadian life, spaces, and institutions can make it seem that there is indeed no racism in Canada.

'Public memory' includes those representations of the past available in mass media, in national and local museums, in public school curricula, in countless monuments and historical plaques. It is evident in the marking of events through public ceremonies, such as those of Remembrance Day. Public memory ranges from the historical accounts available for sale in the local interest sections of bookstores across the country to the monument to Samuel de Champlain overlooking the Ottawa River near the Parliament Buildings. Ordinary people participate in public memory through such things as wearing poppies and watching nationalistic commercials for beer.

Public memory is one of the key ways of making what Benedict Anderson has called 'the imagined community' of the nation.[1] An incident I witnessed a few years ago in Lethbridge, Alberta, illustrates imagined community at work. I happened to be in downtown Lethbridge when the Toronto Blue Jays won the World Series for the first time. People who had been watching the game in the downtown bars poured out onto the streets, got into their cars, and spontaneously drove up and down, honking their horns, waving Canadian flags, and shouting, 'We won! We won!' Imagined community is this 'we.' The good people of Lethbridge had not in any way materially contributed to the Blue Jay's victory, yet because the Blue Jays stood for the nation, they were able to claim the victory as their own, even though it was an event that had taken place in a city 4,000 kilometres away and involved a small group of highly paid professional American athletes.

Participating in acts of public memory is one way of linking people as if they were members of the same community while simultaneously marking certain spaces as quintessentially Canadian. In this marking, Canadian people, spaces, and things are set apart from those of other nations – especially, in the Canadian context, from those of the great Other to the south, the United States. The problem with imagined community is that if some people are imagined as within the community, as belonging to the nation, others are imagined as being outside of it, inexorable aliens who are not and cannot be like one's self. The result is that people can feel connections to strangers living thousands of kilometres away and yet see neighbours living up the street as strangers. Just as public memory helps to foster a sense of connection, so too it fosters a sense of disconnection. If certain people and things are thought to be Canadian and others not, it is because lived histories have associated particular representations and particular physical characteristics with being Canadian. Indeed, this has occurred to the point where these associations have become normal and taken-for-granted, part of our frameworks for understanding the world.

Public memory supplies historical accounts that make it seem both normal and natural that certain things are associated with Canada (for example, maple syrup rather than chopsticks). It does so by recurrently giving voice to a particular interpretation of the past best characterized as 'nationalist grand narrative.'[2] Grand narrative is the stuff of the most widely circulated, 'commonsense' representations, of the CBC's *Canada: A People's History*, of TV commercials, of innumerable school textbooks and speeches by political leaders. It is at once familiar and, in Canadian contexts, continually at risk of colonization by American representations. It is the version of the past that most Canadians resisted learning in high school.

The many variations of grand narrative share certain features. First, within English-Canadian grand narrative, history proper begins with the arrival of Europeans, currently most often with Leif Ericsson and the Vikings. Second, grand narrative almost completely disregards non-Europeans and focuses on the progress of European resettlement, emphasizing 'nation building' by far-seeing 'great men' and even, today, the occasional 'great woman.' The Confederation of four British North American colonies in 1867 is taken as its major turning point, and non-Europeans, such as Louis Riel or Elijah Harper, seem only to intrude when they block European progress. Third, despite its narrative form that moves forward in time from the moment of European arrival, in fact grand narrative imposes an organization on the past that starts with the present and works backwards. In so doing, the narrative makes the present dominance of Europeans seem inevitable and natural. Finally, as the Vancouver historian Daniel Francis has shown, English-Canadian grand narrative is premised on a series of exclusions, the marginalization of Aboriginal people, the infantilization of people from Quebec, and the exclusion of Africans and Asians, but because it is always told from the point of view of English Canadians of British origins, these exclusions are obscured.[3]

Like all historical accounts, grand narrative is an interpretation, a particular account whose origins can be traced to the late nineteenth century and that was popularized in the early twentieth century through public school curricula. However, to many people grand narrative is *the real past, the* history of Canada. Canadian history may start with the Vikings, but this is because that is the way the past really was.

Grand narrative is not particularly good history, as it often fails to represent events within the contexts that actually produced them. For example, the fixation on Europeans ignores the fact that in the first three hundred or so years of what is usually taken to be Canada's history, up until about 1800, Europeans were at best minor players in the territory now called Canada, and were confined to the St Lawrence basin and a few outposts on the edge of the Great Lakes and the Atlantic coast. Until that time, Aboriginal peoples were the overwhelming majority of the population in the territory that is today called Canada. In parts of that territory, they remained dominant throughout the nineteenth and twentieth centuries, as indeed they remain in some places today.

Yet it is the exploits of the European minority that gain the greatest historical attention, and only rarely are their interconnections to Aboriginal people explored, let alone their interconnections to other people and other places. For example, for over one hundred years, accounts of British Columbia's history have traced the origins of that province to the European fur traders who started arriving at the end of the eighteenth century. Despite the fact that, for most of the nineteenth century, Europeans were a minority of the population, they still get most of the attention. For example, at the time that the colony of Vancouver Island was formally established in 1849, the non-Aboriginal population of 'British Columbia' was perhaps five hundred, in contrast to an Aboriginal population of several hundred thousand. Among other things, the standard narrative obscures the fact that nineteenth-century Europeans were only too well aware that they were in an Aboriginal territory, something that the government of British Columbia apparently has yet to learn.

As I tell my students, this Eurocentric view of Canadian history is a bit like the 1950s science fiction movie *The Blob*, but told from the Blob's point of view. Like the gelatinous substance of the movie, the blob of European resettlement grows from a few tiny outposts to a gigantic entity absorbing everything in its path. Today it is only the Blob that is remembered, because the story of the past is most often told from the point of view of those within it. What has been squished on the outside is unknown or at least untold.

Public memory's reliance on grand narrative makes it unable to represent people's lived histories of racism, while at the same time obscuring the artificiality of its representations. I would like to illustrate this with three specific examples. The first describes some of the problematic assumptions of grand narrative and the ease with which these assumptions foster exclusions. The second illustrates that multicultural add-ons to the grand narrative do not fundamentally alter its terms. The third illustrates the inability of grand narrative frameworks to give an adequate account of racism. I should note that my interest here is less to criticize those responsible for the particular representations that I will discuss than it is to suggest that we are dealing with a cultural pattern of exclusion, part of our taken-for-granted understandings of the categories that frame who and what is Canadian and who and what is not, and hence whose history counts and why. The resulting inclusions and exclusions racialize people living in Canada – that is, they make normal the idea that there are innately different kinds of people who can be sorted hierarchically on a scale from the most Canadian to the least, from those who naturally and unproblematically belong in the country to those who do not.

My first example is the 2001 Dominion Institute/Ipsos-Reid Canada Day survey.[4] To me the survey and its questions illustrate the taken-for-granted framework of grand narrative and the ease with which this framework fosters exclusions. The very first question in the 2001 survey asked, 'Who was the first Prime Minister of Canada?' This seems an entirely reasonable question and is the sort of thing one would expect an educated citizenry to know. However, the common sense answer, John A. Macdonald, is not the obvious fact one might assume. This answer makes sense only if you accept that 'Canada' is the state first organized by the British North America Act of 1867 and that continues into the present day. Significantly, Macdonald was not usually called 'prime minister' in his day nor was he the first head of government of a political entity called 'Canada.' That honour goes to Louis-Hippolyte LaFontaine, who became premier of the Province of Canada in 1840. Thus, far from being the only 'correct' answer, a simple and unproblematic fact, the answer 'Macdonald' is an interpretation. It is correct only within the logic of a particular narrative that sees Canada as the nation-state that formally begins in 1867.

Grand narrative is more about the nation as a kind of naturally occurring and unquestioned category than it is about the actual state called 'Canada.' This is shown by another question, 'Name one of the wars in which Canada was invaded by the United States?' If we conceive Canada as the political entity founded in 1867, the answer is that it has never been invaded by the United States, but because the answers being sought are the War of American Independence and the War of 1812, 'Canada' is apparently more than the nation-state and predates Confederation. (In which case, why isn't the answer to the first question LaFontaine?) Here we see 'the Blob' approach to history. In effect, Canadian history is being equated with European resettlement, not the facts of the nation-state. 'The Blob' may change its colours in 1867, but it apparently starts earlier.

The last question in the survey shows how easy it is for taken-for-granted categories to create exclusions and how grand narrative naturalizes categories of Canadian-ness by excluding various people from public memory. The question is, 'In what decade in the 20th century were Canadian women given the right to vote in elections?' Here, the answer being looked for is the 1910s. Again this answer appears to make complete sense as it was indeed in this decade that the federal government and most provinces extended voting rights at general elections to women for the first time since 1867. However, in fact, this answer reduces 'Canadians' to English-speaking people of European origins. Women in Quebec got the right to vote in 1940, but in the logic of this question and answer they apparently are not 'Canadian.' Nor are the Chinese, Japanese, and South Asian women 'Canadian' who (along with their menfolk) got the right to vote federally and in certain provinces only in 1947–9. Nor, presumably, are the women 'Canadian' who were so-called status Indians and who did not get the right to vote federally until 1960, when all 'status Indians' did. Similarly, the category 'Canadian women' apparently does not include the women of the Iroquois Confederacy, who had been voting since at least the thirteenth century, only to have this right taken away by the Canadian government in the twentieth.

Now, it might seem that my concerns here are largely a matter of semantics, the difference between calling someone a 'prime minister' and a 'premier.' But the problem of grand narrative ceases to be merely semantic when the categories and assumptions at work within it mean that young people are confronted with curricula that define some of them as 'Canadian,' those whose great-grandmothers got the right to vote in the 1910s, and defines others as non-Canadian, those whose great-grandmothers did not. This has profound consequences. For example, many African-Canadian students disengage from school in part because they rarely see themselves represented by the curriculum. For these young people, school is about and for racialized white people.[5]

The problem has been eloquently put by Denise, an African-Canadian student who spoke of her reasons for leaving school in a study conducted by the sociologist George Dei and his colleagues. According to Denise, 'The curriculum ... was one-sided, especially when it came down to history. There was never a mention of any Black people that have contributed to society ... I mean, everything, it's the White man that did. History is just based on the European Canadian that came over.' Denise's feelings were echoed by Darren, another student in the study: 'It's like you're learning about somebody else's history: you're learning about when they discovered America when things were good for them and when they did this and when they did that ... It started to take its toll on me after a while.'[6] Similarly, few First Nations students are likely to identify with a curriculum that begins with the exclusion of their peoples and continues by treating them as little more than the scenery, or as disrupters of the inevitable national progress.

For young people like Denise and Darren, the Canada of the Dominion Institute survey is a foreign country, a place that does not include them, and seems unwilling to do so. Instead of being part of the imagined community, they are excluded from it: they are excluded from its imagining and all too often excluded from its reality. The term for such exclusion is racism.

It would be unfair to lay all of the ills of grand narrative and of systemic racisms at the feet of a private organization that has as its purpose the promotion of historical knowledge, an entirely worthy goal that I fully support. It is therefore significant that similar exclusions get enacted by the historical representations of a much better-funded public institution, the Canadian Museum of Civilization. The Canadian Museum of Civilization has a mandate to represent Canadians in their cultural plurality. It does so through its temporary exhibits, and tries to do so through its permanent displays as well. It is the permanent exhibits that concern me here. As visitors to the museum know, the first floor opens up into a grand gallery that contains a truly magnificent display of six longhouses from Northwest Coast First Nations. Symbolically it establishes first peoples as the basis for Canadian civilization and makes imagined community by linking Ottawa to the British Columbia coast, five thousand kilometres away. But in doing so, it also fixes first peoples as literally outside of history. This is despite the fact that (as the fine print on the exhibit explains) what is being represented in the hall is in fact historical (dating from the mid- to late nineteenth century). While today many coastal communities have longhouses that they use for such things as community centres, no one, insofar as I know, actually lives in them anymore. Thus, what is being presented as the life of Northwest Coast peoples is in fact something extracted from and frozen in time.[7]

History proper begins with the Canada Hall on the third floor and a walkthrough of 'Canadian History.' Predictably, this exhibit starts with a diorama on the Vikings and continues to focus on Europeans. Visitors walk through a fortified gate and an inn from New France and buildings from a turn-of-the-twentieth-century Ontario town. Significantly, the museum tries hard to represent the multi-ethnic character of Canada. The exhibit also includes displays on Metis buffalo hunters, a Ukrainian church, and a Chinese hand laundry. This latter exhibit was opened only in October 2000.[7]

However, despite these efforts at inclusion, the cumulative effect of this walkthrough is that the history of Canada is still a European affair. For example, the chronology it relates literally moves geographically from east to west and from south to north, following the progress of the European frontier. It links the resettlement of Canada to Europe; hence the displays on initial European colonizers – Vikings and Basque whalers – even though there is no continuity between their settlements and Canada today. In the Blob's-eye view of the past that emerges, one would not know about African slavery in Canada nor about the African Loyalists of Nova Scotia and New Brunswick. Visitors would have no knowledge of government policies to force First Nations to accept treaties and empty the land for European resettlement or about the one hundred years of immigration policies designed to make Canada 'white' and to keep African and Asian people out, or of the protracted anti-Semitism of a country based on a fundamentally Christian vision. Even the Chinese laundry exhibit, which pulls few punches and acknowledges the discrimination and isolation that many Chinese men in Canada faced, presents an interpretation that redeems the national past. As the museum's website tells visitors, 'To many of the laundrymen's descendants, the hand laundry is a symbol not only of hardship but of survival, endurance, patience and sacrifice for the future.'[9] The museum is silent on the men who were broken by the experience, who returned to China, who starved to death, who did not endure. Nor does it record the reality of what such experiences meant for the women and children of these laundry workers, who were legally not allowed to come to Canada.[10]

Given that the Museum of Civilization is designed to make visitors to the national capital feel good about Canada, it is perhaps no surprise that the darker aspects of Canadian history are not fully acknowledged there. The museum cannot do everything, and its purpose is to instil a sense of Canadian nationalism, not to explain Canadian racism. The fact that these two things are mutually exclusive illustrates my point. Apparently we can use history to foster nationalism or we can use it to foster anti-racism, but not both. In the end, the museum demonstrates that simply grafting a Chinese- or an African-Canadian chapter onto the overall grand narrative does not fundamentally alter its terms. While such additions may create spaces that allow alternate representations, they are unlikely to be of sufficient weight to counter the normalizing of grand narrative. In the walkthrough of Canadian history, history still starts with Europeans, even if it recognizes some non-European late arrivals. Add-ons also cannot address the problem that those who do not have long-lived roots in the country still get constituted as outsiders.

Even well-intentioned efforts to include certain groups can lead to symbolic ghettoization. For example, in public schools, the histories of African Canadians are often ghettoized into Black History Month. There is nothing wrong with Black History Month per se, but there is a great deal wrong with it being the only time of the year when African-Canadian experiences are represented. Similarly, the contributions of Chinese workers in building the Canadian Pacific Railway might be celebrated as a Chinese contribution to 'the National Dream,' but if this is the only story told about Chinese in Canada, their arguably much more significant contribution to national life – their largely successful fight against racist exclusion and for full democratic rights – is excluded. Nor is 'multiculturalizing' an otherwise unicultural curriculum to include the contributions of various cultural groups a complete solution. In schools where English or French is the native tongue of only a minority of students, or where most do not come from European backgrounds, or have not lived in Canada long, as indeed is common in many parts of Canada, inevitably someone will be left out, if only because his or her cultural group has been the last to arrive, too late to be included in the textbook, the curriculum guide, or in that day's lesson plan.

All of this leads me to think that we need to dramatically re-imagine our approaches to the past, both approaches to public memory and to history teaching. To give you a sense of how dramatic a break is needed, I would like to turn to a third example of public memory, the critically constructed, first-year university Canadian history survey text by Margaret Conrad and Alvin Finkel, *History of the Canadian Peoples*. A first-rate survey textbook of this kind synthesizes a field of historical research. As such it presents a kind of snapshot of a broader pattern of historical representation. This text, being published in its fourth edition in 2006, is a generally successful synthesis of what has been called the new social history with the not-so-new political history. Its excellent didactic qualities, time lines, discussions of historiographic controversies, detailed lists of additional readings, and accompanying CD-Roms all make it a work of high quality and the text that I usually use to introduce people to Canadian history. Reworked in multiple editions, it has become increasingly multicultural, as it incorporates discussions on such matters as Black Loyalists or Aboriginal people in the fur trade and goes to some lengths to present the voices of members of previously excluded communities. However, *History of the Canadian Peoples* does not escape the framework of grand narrative. It continues the focus on Europeans, who remain the main story. It preserves Confederation in 1867 as its major organizational division, separating volumes one from two.* Discussions of the European context for migration link Canadian history to Europe, but no equivalent discussions link Canada to other places. Meanwhile, the Aboriginal societies that until the nineteenth century were the majority population in Canada and that continue to occupy much of its land mass are reduced to minor roles. After an initial account of Aboriginal societies, Aboriginal people enter into *History of the Canadian Peoples* only insofar as they interact with Europeans and their purposes – for example, in the Riel Rebellion or Elijah Harper's blocking of the Meech Lake Accord. Although First Nations people, Black/African and Asian Canadians appear as the subjects of white

---

*Not considered here is the role played by the publisher in such decisions. And publishers arguably play a pivotal role in shaping some key historiographical and epistemological issues. In commercial publishing, editorial and marketing departments routinely influence such factors as where to break multivolume texts. Such decisions usually reflect the findings of market researchers into the apparent preferences of professors, many of whom teach Canadian survey courses that still break at Confederation. At the same time, some teachers claim that their courses' chronological parameters are influenced by available textbooks. The issue of the role of the publisher has not received great attention from scholars, but it is an element in the construction of school and college textbooks. For a discussion of the role of textbooks in Canadian history education, see Margaret Conrad and Alvin Finkel, 'Textbook Wars: Canadian Style,' *Canadian Issues*, October 2003. – Ed.

racism, they are not discussed either as active participants in Canadian society in their own right or as peoples whose exclusion was integral to shaping that society. Racism is reduced to isolated incidents or pieces of legislation and often quite literally to sidebars to the main story of European progress. For example, the second volume of the 2002 edition contains a number of passing references to racialized Chinese people as the objects of anti-Chinese feelings or as the builders of the CPR. Only two Chinese people, the Ottawa-based writer Denise Chong and her mother, are mentioned by name.[11]

It might be argued that my criticism here is unfair. After all, some people might say, the Chinese were not really all that important and until recently were a relatively small part of the Canadian population. Nevertheless, the failure to account adequately for the historical experiences of those such as the racialized Chinese people who experienced racist exclusion obscures the fact that Canadian political and social spaces have been formed by the racist exclusion of some people and the equally racist inclusion of others. For example, if in the first half of the twentieth century, virtually every community of any size had its Chinese laundry, as indeed the Museum of Civilization exhibit attempts to show, it means that every community in Canada was racially structured, divided into those who had rights because they belonged to one racialized group and those who did not have these rights because they belonged to another. That the very rights and privileges guaranteed in the Charter of Rights and Freedoms are there for all citizens to enjoy, not because some far-seeing politicians granted them, but because for decades people of Chinese and other origins fought for them, seems to me to be a not insignificant thing for people to know about their national past.

If *History of the Canadian Peoples*, a critically written scholarly text, fails to explain or adequately describe the racism of Canada's past, how much more so must it be likely that public school texts also fail. After all, these latter are severely constrained by mandated curricula and the public acceptability of certain themes.

To fully appreciate the extent to which public memory in Canada fails to give an account of racism in Canada, I would like to give a brief overview of the history of anti-Chinese racism. My purpose in doing so is not to reduce the Chinese experience in Canada to racism only, but rather to highlight the extent to which such a history cannot be contained within grand narratives' celebration of European colonization. Through my account of anti-Chinese racism, I also hope to show the inadequacies of accounts of racism that reduce it to the exceptional or to individual prejudice. For those who are aware of Canada only as represented in grand narrative, it may seem that the history I am now going to describe is of some unknown foreign country. I should point out that although I focus here on anti-Chinese racism, equally disturbing tales could be told of the historical experiences of African Canadians, of other Asian Canadians, of First Nations, Inuit, and Metis peoples, and of Jewish people in Canada.

The Chinese were such a significant group in the history of nine-teenth-century British Columbia that the noted historical geographer, Cole Harris, and his colleague Robert Galois have argued that this history can be understood only by taking into account the presence of three conglomerate groups, First Nations, Europeans, and Chinese.[12] Indeed, at British Columbia's entry into Confederation in 1871, the Chinese were as significant a group as Europeans, having been in the territory continuously since the 1858 gold rush. They were such a significant population that the European resettlers of British Columbia deliberately created a state system that limited or kept out so-called Chinese. Thus, in 1872, one of the first acts of the British Columbia legislature took away the right to vote from anyone of 'Chinese race' as well as any 'aborginee of North America.' By 1912, by one count, 114 separate pieces of provincial legislation curtailed the rights of the Chinese and other Asians.[13] People identified as of Chinese race were barred from working for the provincial government, for its licensees, Crown corporations, and provincially incorporated companies. They were barred from serving on juries, from practising law, and at times from being licensed as teachers. An array of municipal regulations subjected them to arbitrary inspection and prevented the Chinese and companies that employed them from bidding on contracts, and from gaining certain business licences. The Chinese were often barred from using public facilities such as swimming pools and restricted to Chinese-only sections in movie theatres. Even the cemeteries of the late nineteenth and early twentieth centuries were racially segregated.

Restrictive legislation was accompanied by popular violence against the Chinese. Perennial sports of Anglo-European youths in Victoria and Vancouver were 'Chink bashing' and 'cart-tipping' (the later involved overturning the carts of Chinese pedlars). Many Euro-Canadian adults also engaged in sustained and organized violence. The most spectacular incident was the 1907 anti-Chinese and anti-Japanese riot in Vancouver that took place following a rally sponsored by the Asiatic

Exclusion League and all fifty-four of the city's white-only trade unions. Fifteen years later, the residents of Canton Alley in Vancouver maintained a heavy metal gate suspended by a rope over the entrance to the alley. Next to the rope, chained to the wall, was a machete that residents could use to cut the rope to keep agitators out in the event of another riot.[14] As Chinese-language newspapers in the 1910s and 1920s record, whole districts of British Columbia, closed down by white mob action and violence, were off limits to Chinese people.[15]

The combined effect of these actions was racial apartheid in British Columbia. The state and state-regulated sectors were established as exclusively for people of European origins, as was much of the territory and almost all the economy. Today it may be that the Chinatowns of Vancouver and Victoria are tourist attractions. One hundred years ago, along with those of Cumberland, Nanaimo, and New Westminster, they were the only safe places for those racialized as Chinese to live. Indeed the pressures of anti-Chinese racism were such that, beginning around 1910, many Chinese left the province for other regions of Canada, becoming the laundry workers of the Museum of Civilization exhibit.

However, Anti-Chinese racism does not end there. Throughout the nineteenth and twentieth centuries, English-language newspapers, magazines, novels, and school textbooks continually racialized Chinese people as aliens, as outsiders to the imagined community of Canada. Let me use, and elaborate on, an example already mentioned by Peter Seixas in chapter 1: the justification used by John A. Macdonald to extend Chinese disenfranchisement to the federal level. In 1885, while Macdonald was debating the Dominion Franchise Act – what he called his 'greatest triumph,' more important than Confederation, more important than the transcontinental railway – he told the House of Commons that the Chinese were 'an Asiatic population, alien in spirit, alien in feeling, alien in everything.' He said that the so-called Chinaman 'has no British instincts or British feelings or aspirations, and therefore ought not to have a vote.'[16] This is a classic example of racialization, of the social invention and marking of race difference. In effect Sir John was fixing the so-called Chinese as alien and, by implication, was fixing the so-called British as native, as people who properly and unquestioningly belonged in the imagined community. The artificiality of this construction is shown by the reactions of some members of the House of Commons, who questioned his characterization of the Chinese, protesting that 'the Chinese' were as good British subjects as he was.

However, Macdonald was not content with taking voting rights away from racialized Chinese. He also imposed an immigration head tax on Chinese workers and their family members. By 1904, this head tax was set at $500, the equivalent of an unskilled worker's annual wages. In 1923 the federal government adopted the Chinese Immigration Act, which not only barred all people of 'Chinese race' from immigrating to Canada, it required those already in the country, including the Canadian-born, to register with the federal government and to obtain a certificate of registration. Failure to produce this certificate on request was made punishable by fines, imprisonment, and deportation. The House of Commons' version of the bill also provided for the deportation of anyone who could not pass an English test, but the Senate quashed this particular measure. Along with so-called status Indians, the Chinese are the only group who have been required to register with the government during peacetime. Significantly, when this legislation was enacted, no members of the House of Commons opposed it. The idea of Chinese alien-ness had become so fixed in people's minds that it was taken for granted.

One of the consequences of this act was that in 1942, when the young Adrienne Poy and her family arrived in Canada, repatriated on a Red Cross ship from wartorn Hong Kong, the only reason she was allowed entry was that her father was an Australian-born British subject who had worked for the Canadian High Commission in Hong Kong and, with the conditions of the war, return to Australia was impossible. Her family was among the handful of Chinese immigrants admitted to Canada between 1923 and 1947. While Adrienne Clarkson eventually became the governor general of Canada, the idea that racialized Chinese somehow do not really belong in this country remains a recurring trope of English-Canadian discourse.

The idea of Chinese alien-ness has become fixed in Anglo-Canadian imaginations. By the early twentieth century, racist representations of the Chinese were so fierce, and so common, that its casual prevalence is shocking to contemporary readers. I will give you one example of this. This is from an 1912 British Columbia magazine devoted to Chamber of Commerce boosterism. An editorial in the magazine describes the so-called Oriental as follows:

> Racially he [the Oriental] is as opposite to the Anglo-Saxon in life, thought, religion, temperament, taste, morals, and modes, as ice is to fire. AND HE CAN NEVER BE OTHERWISE ... He cannot be changed, even by centuries of contact, any more than the leopard can change his spots. He may adopt

certain of the white man's vices, because to him these seem virtues; but he will not take up any of the white race's virtues, because these seem, either as vices to him or negligible trifles.[17]

Here racial difference is presented as fixed, a matter of fundamentally different and mutually exclusive moral qualities.

Similar views that the Chinese did not really belong in Canada were propagated by school textbooks, as we can see in the example of a 1929 elementary social studies text by Donalda Dickie, one of the pioneers of children's literature in Canada. This text introduced young readers to children in Canada from multiple ethnic backgrounds. Thus we meet Little Buffalo Calf, who is going to participate in the Indian parade of the local fair; we meet Billy, 'the brave Canadian boy,' who, even though he is injured, stops the horses from eating the oats after they break through the fence. We even meet William and Wilhemina, who are 'New Canadians' from the Netherlands. Then we meet Poy, 'a Chinese boy.' We are told that Poy is 'a visitor to Canada.' To be sure we are also told, 'Poy works hard.' It seems that he helps his parents with their market-gardening business, but according to the text his family is sav-ing 'all of their money' and one day will 'go home' to China: 'Then Poy will have a good time. He will bring out his kite and fly it all afternoon.' It seems that the Chinese can truly be happy only in China.[18]

We see the idea that Chinese Canadians are foreigners who don't really belong in Canada reappearing in 1979 when CTV's program *W5* broadcast a story alleging that places at Canadian universities were being taken away from Canadian students. Whenever they showed supposed foreigners, they showed Chinese faces. In the early 1990s, people in Richmond, BC, became upset at what they saw as the inva-sion of Chinese into their neighbourhood, when a local mall catering to recent immigrants from Hong Kong distributed a flyer written only in Chinese. People complained about this 'foreign language.' At the time, Chinese had been spoken and written continuously in the region for one hundred and forty years – as long as English has been. One won-ders how long it takes for a language to become Canadian.

The racism of this history I have recounted is not simply prejudice. Rather it is a pattern of life in which racism defined where and with whom people lived, where they could work or go to school, where they were buried. This racism was not exceptional. It was on-going. It was so prevalent a pattern that it affected not only Chinese Canadians but

European Canadians as well. It is also a racism that has continued into the present.

Rather than trying to get people to learn the grand narrative or to memorize the key landmarks of a narrative that excludes many of them while making others dominant, we need to re-imagine our approach to history education. This re-imagining begins with a recognition that not everyone enters our common spaces under conditions of equality. Some enter with their right to be in these spaces unchallenged, their histories well known. Others enter with histories that are unknown, submerged under the weight of widespread representations that exclude them. Still others enter with histories that have been lived in other places. The anti-racist task is to make these histories visible in all their complexities.

In re-imagining history education, the first challenge is to enable each one of us to explore his or her own past, to construct a narrative that explains how it is that we come to inhabit common spaces, and to allow others to see and engage with these narratives. A second challenge is to help people see how their personal histories intertwine with those of the multiple communities to which they are connected, with the people of their immediate neighbourhoods, their places of work, their ethnic and religious communities, the people on their soccer team, and the people in the communities on the other side of the world to whom they are also linked. A third task is to provide all of us with a sense of how the spaces we inhabit have been constructed by people who have gone before. These spaces range from Much Music to the local shopping mall. Some of these spaces are even nationalist ones. Through such a re-imagining of history, by replacing the monolith of grand narrative with a web of multiple overlapping histories, we can help to insure that the real communities in which we live, rather than racisms, endure.

NOTES

1 Benedict Anderson, *Imagined Communities: Reflections on the Origin and Spread of Nationalism* (London: Verso, 1983).
2 Allan Megill, '"Grand Narrative" and the Discipline of History,' in Frank Ankersmit and Hans Kellner, eds, *A New Philosophy of History* (Chicago: University of Chicago Press, 1995), 151–73, and Dorothy Ross, 'Grand Narrative in American Historical Writing: From Romance to Uncertainty,' *American Historical Review* 100, 3 (1995): 651–77. See also Timothy J. Stanley,

'Why I Killed Canadian History: Conditions for an Anti-Racist History in Canada,' *Histoire sociale/Social History* 33, 65 (2001): 79–103.

3 Daniel Francis, *National Dreams: Myth, Memory, and Canadian History* (Vancouver: Arsenal Pulp Press, 1997).

4 See Dominion Institute / Ipsos-Reid Poll, '5th Annual Canada Day History Quiz,' http://www.ipsos-na.com/news/pressrelease.cfm?id=1255 (accessed 14 September 2005).

5 An all too common view. Njoki N. Wane and Erica Neegan, 'African Canadian High School Girls and Their Quest for Education,' *Orbit* 34, 1 (2005): 36.

6 George J. Sefa Dei, Josephine Mazzuca, Elizabeth McIsaac, Jasmin Zine, *Reconstructing 'Drop-out': A Critical Ethnography of the Dynamics of Black Students' Disengagement from School* (Toronto: University of Toronto Press, 1998), 138.

7 See Canadian Museum of Civilization, 'Grand Hall,' 15 June 2004. http://www.civilization.ca/aborig/grand/grandeng.html (accessed 14 September 2005).

8 Canadian Museum of Civilization, 'Canada Hall,' 27 September 2001, http://www.civilization.ca/hist/canp1/canp1eng.html (accessed 15 September 2005).

9 Canadian Museum of Civilization, 'Enduring Hardship – Chinese Hand Laundry,' 16 March 2005, http://www.civilization.ca/hist/phase2/mod5e.html (accessed 14 September 2005).

10 By contrast, the publication prepared to accompany the exhibit does make these points. See Ban Seng Hoe, *Enduring Hardship: The Chinese Laundry in Canada* (Gatineau, QC: Museum of Civilization, 2003).

11 See Margaret Conrad and Alvin Finkel, *History of the Canadian Peoples*, 2nd ed., 2 vols. (Toronto: Copp Clark, 1998) and especially, volume 2. The text reproduces a quote from Denise Chong's account of her own family's history, *The Concubine's Children: Portrait of a Family Divided* (Toronto: Penguin Books Canada, 1994).

12 Robert Galois and R. Cole Harris, 'Recalibrating Society: The Population Geography of British Columbia,' *Canadian Geographer* 38, 1 (1994): 37–53.

13 Bruce Ryder, 'Racism and the Constitution: The Constitutional Fate of British Columbia Anti-Asian Legislation, 1884–1909,' *Osgoode Hall Law Journal* 29, 3 (1991): 619–76.

14 Sing Lim, *West Coast Chinese Boy* (Montreal: Tundra Press, 1979).

15 See, especially, *Da Han Gong Bao or The Chinese Times*. The principal histories of Chinese people in Canada remain David T.H. Lee [Lee T'ung-hai], *Jianada Huaqiao shi* [A History of Chinese in Canada] (Taibei: Zhonghua Da

Dian Bianying Hui, 1967); Edgar Wickberg, ed., *From China to Canada: A History of the Chinese Communities of Canada* (Toronto: McClelland and Stewart, 1982); Anthony B. Chan, *Gold Mountain: The Chinese in the New World* (Vancouver: New Star Books, 1983); and Peter S. Li, *The Chinese in Canada* (Toronto: Oxford University Press, 1988). See also Wing Chung Ng, *The Chinese in Vancouver, 1945–1980: The Pursuit of Identity and Power* (Vancouver: UBC Press, 1999) and David Chuenyan Lai, *Chinatowns: Towns within Cities in Canada* (Vancouver: UBC Press, 1988).

16 Canada, House of Commons, *Debates*, 4 May 1885, 1589 and 1582.

17 Ernest McGaffey, 'British Columbia and the Yellow Man,' *British Columbia Magazine* 8, 3 (March 1912): 198.

18 D.J. Dickie, *All about Canada for Little Folks* (Toronto: J.M. Dent, 1929).

4 History, Humanistic Education, and Participatory Democracy

KEITH C. BARTON

A few years ago I was interviewing Susan and Jean, two Kentucky girls who were around 10 or 11 years old, about their ideas regarding history.

INTERVIEWER: Why do you think history is something people study?
JEAN: Because it's probably interesting, because *I* think it's interesting.
INTERVIEWER: Why do you think it's interesting?
SUSAN: [So you can] know what the world was like back then compared to now.
JEAN: I would usually find it more interesting because of the cars, and the women – how, like, women [got the right] to vote.
INTERVIEWER: So what do you think makes that interesting?
JEAN: Because it tells what happened then, to now, and [you can] see what things are today, because some people back then made them.
SUSAN: I just think that it's just interesting, it's things that you can tell your kids when you get older.
JEAN: It's like a tradition.

These girls, who had not even finished elementary school, had already developed a rationale for studying history, one that involved learning how people in the past had brought about societal changes that affected them today – such as women gaining the right to vote – and they had also thought about their own responsibility for passing along that information some day.

A few years later, I spent several months talking to children in Northern Ireland about history. When I asked Nuala, a ten-year-old girl there, why she thought history was something they studied in school, she explained, 'It's very interesting because you learn what other people used to live like, not what *we* used to live like, and what they used to wear and how they used to act and all ... because now we know how people act, but we didn't know how they act, and it's very interesting finding out about other people.' Nuala, like many of the children I talked to in Northern Ireland, had also developed clear ideas about why history was worth studying, particularly its role in understanding the lives of people different from those she already knew about.

Let me share one more quote. This one came from Daniel, a slightly older child, about twelve or thirteen years old, also from Northern Ireland. I had been talking to him about why history is important outside school, and like most secondary students there he was well aware of the sectarian uses of history in his community. But then I asked him about history at school, and how that might be different from other kinds of history. Daniel explained, 'When you learn history [at school], you can learn to understand more and be more appreciative of what people think and what they believe in, because it doesn't help you if you just believe one thing and think everyone else is wrong.' Many of the secondary students I talked to in Northern Ireland gave explanations similar to Daniel's – they thought learning history at school would give them the chance to critically examine the accepted beliefs of their community and to make up their own minds about history.

I've interviewed hundreds of students, in both the United States and Northern Ireland, and asked them their ideas about history. Among the questions I always ask are 'Why do you think people care about history?' and usually 'Why do you think history is a subject at school?' Teachers don't usually discuss the purpose of studying history with their students in either Northern Ireland or the United States. Only a very small portion of the children I've interviewed have said that this is something they've talked about in class, and many of them have scoffed at the idea that history teachers – or any other teachers, for that matter – would let them in on the rationale behind their subject.

From my perspective as a researcher into children's thinking, this lack of attention to history's purpose is actually a distinct advantage, because it means that when I talk to children, I'm not just hearing some kind of imperfect rehearsal of maxims picked up from their teachers or from others. Instead, I'm hearing the explanations that children themselves have begun to develop about the reasons for learning history.

And these explanations typically reflect the range of purposes we find in adult society: some children note that learning history might be important in case people had historical hobbies such as genealogy, if they wanted to work in a museum or planned to become a teacher, or in case they were ever on a quiz show. But as the quotes I've just shared indicate, some students – a great many in fact – have developed more sophisticated explanations for why history is a valuable form of knowledge. Each of these quotes suggests that learning history has a social – or even political – purpose. I would argue that these children have begun to develop expectations for history that closely mirror the subject's most important contributions to contemporary society, and that educators would benefit from considering these purposes in greater detail. Towards that end, I want to explore the social purposes of history and to suggest some implications of those for what we do in school or other educational settings. Most of my observations will focus on schools and students and teachers, because those are the contexts I'm most familiar with, but much of what I have to say would be just as applicable to history in any public setting, such as museums or the media.[1]

It may require some justification for me to suggest that history in school should even have a purpose, much less that the purpose should be social or political in nature. In Northern Ireland, teachers and other educators sometimes claim that history is solely an academic subject, and that its place in the curriculum is justified by ... well, by the fact that it's in the curriculum. The purpose of teaching history, some claim, is to enable students to pass their examinations in history. These educators don't expect or desire that history should have any justification other than the fact that it's an established part of schooling. In the United States, students in most states haven't traditionally been tested in history, and so a somewhat different version of this argument is usually put forth – namely, that history should be studied 'for its own sake.' I've never been able to work out exactly what that means, even at a grammatical level – I don't think I could diagram that phrase if it were used in a sentence. I don't know just what the 'sake' of history is, or how history itself could exert some agency that deserves our attention. When people refer to studying history for its own sake, they may be trying to associate the subject with other supernatural forces with whose sake we should be concerned – Christ's sake, Pete's sake, heaven's sake, and so on. My point is that for many people, in Britain and North America, history just *is*, and there's no point in wasting our time trying to figure out why it's worth studying.

But history's place in the curriculum requires – and deserves – some higher purpose than the self-justifying ones of helping students pass exams or studying it for its own sake. History has to be justified in part because there is no neutral or so-called 'objective' approach to history, or to history education. We have to make choices – choices about what history to study, and how to study it. We can't study everything that ever happened in the past, and we can't use all possible methods in studying it. Do we emphasize wars and politics, or daily life and social relations? Do we teach about great heroes, or common people? Do we tell stories to students, or have them investigate questions? Do we start with the distant past and work forward, or begin with contemporary issues and trace their origins? There's no objective basis for making these choices; they depend on what we want to accomplish with history.

Even if we agree on a list of topics to be covered, we have to decide what we and our students should do with those topics. The study of the Columbian encounter, for example, may take place as part of a dispassionate examination of how human societies interact, a judgmental indictment of European conquest, or a modern 'creation myth' that establishes a sense of identity for North Americans. Similarly, the Irish famine can represent part of a scholarly explanation for immigration to North America, a politically motivated example of British indifference to Irish suffering, or memorized fodder for an exam question. Everyone makes these choices, whether as a historian, museum curator, textbook publisher, school board, or teacher; we focus on some things, and we leave others out. We need to think carefully about the implications of these choices and whether they truly support the goals we have for history education. Without a clear rationale for why we teach history, such choices are going to be made on the basis of convenience, or tradition, or economics.

Everyone who has an opinion about history education implicitly recognizes that history can be used for more than one purpose, and that therefore choices have to be made. Often, people make a distinction between 'history' and 'the past,' or between 'professional history' and 'amateur history,' or between 'history' and 'heritage,' or that old favorite, between 'the use of history' and 'the abuse of history.' Anyone who makes these distinctions is admitting that there's more than one way of approaching the past, but most go out of their way to dismiss any approach that isn't their favorite – and their favorite is almost always synonymous with the work of professional, academic historians in universities. All those other approaches aren't *really* history – they're just 'the past' or 'heritage' or 'amateur' or 'abuses.' That kind of argument avoids serious discussion about the purpose of history. In fact, it ultimately suppresses such discussion: it limits debate by defining what 'real' history is and dismissing everything else. And if there's only one kind of history that counts as 'real,' then discussing its purpose is superfluous. The task for educators would simply be to toe the line and teach students what real historians do.

This assertion that some kinds of history are real, and that all the others are fake, might be appropriate if we lived in a dictatorship, or if schools existed only to produce professional historians, but they're hardly appropriate for the kinds of broad education found in countries such as the United States, Canada, and Britain. We have to begin not with definitions of what history is and is not, but by carefully considering the purpose of teaching history. Then we can develop a course of history education that supports that purpose. The criterion for determining what history should be taught (and how) is not whether it conforms to some know-it-all's definition of history but whether it serves the purposes we have for the subject.

In the United States, I would be on somewhat safe ground with this assertion. Unlike in Britain, in the United States we haven't usually justified public education on narrow academic grounds, but rather on its contribution to an educated citizenry. The very institution of schooling in the United States, as well as the subjects that are studied at school, are expected to contribute to democratic citizenship, and we have a long tradition of theorizing about the nature of education for democracy. So in considering the purposes of history education, I begin with the assumption that it should contribute to citizenship.

However, I immediately have to clarify just what I mean by education for citizenship. The term 'citizenship education' has recently become popular – or maybe I should say unpopular – in Britain. There have been mandates for British schools to prepare students for citizenship and for each subject area to consider its potential contribution to this effort. In a country such as Britain, where citizenship hasn't traditionally been part of the explicit purpose of schooling, many educators have found this perspective troubling. The word 'citizenship,' for many, seems to call up images of old-fashioned imperialists, men marching off in pith helmets and khakis to colonize yet another corner of the globe, or, more to the point, their modern equivalent: unthinking supporters of the British government's involvement in Iraq or other dodgy adventures inspired by the U.S. quest for world domination. If this were the meaning of citizenship, then I too would be worried.

In the United States, the term 'citizenship' sometimes has similar connotations, particularly after the events of September 11th: some people equate it with a sort of conservative patriotism – middle-aged men with American flag pins in their lapels, or essay contests sponsored by the Daughters of the American Revolution. But I think most educators in the United States would recognize the distinction between citizenship and either patriotism or nationalism. They wouldn't think of citizenship education as being about the promotion of a particular set of pro-government attitudes, but as being a matter of teaching students about their rights and responsibilities as members of a representative democracy. In operation, this is a curriculum that teaches students how the government works – how congressional districts are apportioned, how a bill becomes law, the right to trial by a jury of peers. This is not citizenship education as nationalism, fortunately, but it may be citizenship education as unremitting boredom – and it is certainly citizenship education that focuses on the private interests of individuals and their interaction with the state.

This view of citizenship is too limited. A number of scholars have argued that this liberal, individual, rights-based view of democracy must give way to a vision of democratic engagement that is more *pluralist*, more *deliberative*, and more *participatory*. Democracy has to become more pluralist because in most Western countries we now live in a pluralist society, one in which there are multiple visions of what constitutes truth, morality, and the good life. No one framework can legitimately command the agreement of everyone in society – not liberalism or fundamentalism or socialism or capitalism or anarchy or any other single perspective. People hold, and are going to continue to hold, radically different perspectives on the issues that require public action, and a liberal, individual view of democracy doesn't do much to enable them to work together in the face of such fundamental differences. A pluralist view of citizenship recognizes that these differences exist and that they can't be ignored or put aside when people come together to make political decisions. Citizens have to learn to engage these differences and to work together with those who have radically different ideas than they do themselves.

This requires a kind of citizenship that places deliberation at its core. People will be able to work together to make decisions only when they have a chance to discuss their differences, explore what they have in common, and reach consensus through the difficult process of mutual engagement and public discourse. Deliberation, though, does not mean practising debate – the competitive scoring of points that's synonymous with much public talk in liberal democracy. Deliberation means reasoning together for the common good.

In a deliberative democracy, individuals don't simply pursue their own material gain or advancement, or seek increased freedom or liberty for their own communities; rather, they seek to contribute to the health of the multiple communities they belong to and intersect with, whether those are local neighborhoods; voluntary associations; larger national, religious, or ethnic groups; or even the global community of humankind and its environment. This concern with the common good is a hallmark of deliberative democracy, and citizens have to be committed to improving not only their own lives, but the lives of their fellow citizens.

I should point out, though, that the term 'common good' sometimes carries the connotation that individual rights, or even self-expression, have to give way to the demands of some collective authority, and that's not what I mean at all. Maybe we'd be better off replacing 'common good' with 'social justice,' which more clearly suggests the need to reconsider existing social arrangements rather than simply expecting citizens to uphold the status quo. But in any event, a critical component of democracy must be this concern with public deliberation in the service of goals broader than those of individual gain.

The third component of democratic citizenship is implied in the other two – namely, the idea that citizens should be actively engaged in making public decisions, rather than delegating these decisions to politicians or experts. This is a view of democracy in which voting is only one of many acts of citizenship, a view in which people take control of their futures through direct participation in the institutions that affect them – not just governmental bodies, but neighbourhood associations, unions, churches, faculties, political parties, charitable organizations, and so on. Politics in a democracy cannot simply be what politicians do, but what we all do as we take charge of our futures.

If we accept that citizenship should be pluralist, deliberative, and participatory, then we have to consider the implications of this view for history education. This is not a matter of asking, 'How can history *produce* good citizens?' I have no illusions that the study of history, or any other subject, is going to single-handedly change the nature of modern politics. The question, instead, is 'How can history *contribute* to democratic citizenship?' or 'What *role* does it have to play in supporting the conditions that allow democracy to flourish?' And perhaps just as importantly, 'What approaches to history education might stand in the way of democracy?'

My answers to these questions come from a source so traditional you may think I'm old-fashioned for even suggesting it. In fact, you may start wondering if I have an American flag pin in my lapel after all. This very traditional source for thinking about how history might contribute to democratic citizenship is humanistic education. 'Humanistic education' isn't a term we hear very much these days. We sometimes hear 'the humanities,' meaning whatever's left over in liberal education once we've taken out the natural and social sciences. But 'humanistic education' has a somewhat broader meaning. It's by no means certain that everyone would agree with my characterization, but I think our understanding of history education would benefit from considering what I take to be the three key elements of humanistic education.

The first is *reasoned judgment*. Humanistic education is associated with developing powers of critical appraisal. Elliot Eisner notes, 'Humanists place a premium on the human's ability to be critically rational, that is, to reason deeply and sensitively about important human matters.' The development of this kind of judgment is also a key requirement for participatory democracy. Because there is no independent ground for political knowledge – no certain truths upon which decisions can be based – action depends on careful reasoning and consideration of evidence. As Benjamin Barber suggests, citizens don't merely *choose*, they *judge* options and possibilities.[2]

How can history contribute to developing reasoned judgment for citizens in a democracy? I think there are two principal ways, both of which are critical to thinking about how history should be taught. The first is by giving students *something to reason about*. By this I mean that history should help students understand that the institutions, attitudes, and social patterns we live with today are the result of historical developments. Our economy, our political system, our cultural beliefs and practices aren't written in stone – they aren't natural, timeless, or universal. They're the products of the past, whether of specific events and decisions or of long-term processes, and if we hope to prepare students to engage in thoughtful discussion of public issues, then we have to help them understand how the past led to the present (including multiple explanations for that relationship). And in fact, this is sometimes taken to be the unique contribution of history, the single characteristic that separates the discipline from sociology, economics, or other social sciences: instead of analysing social patterns at a single moment, history traces the development of those patterns over time.

This idea seems to be part of Susan's and Jean's comments that I shared at the beginning: They think history is interesting because it helps them understand how current societal arrangements – such as women being able to vote – came about. And many students in Northern Ireland are very consciously aware that history can serve this purpose. The secondary students I've interviewed there often explain the need to explore the historical roots of modern problems, and they expect that school will help them understand how the present-day Troubles came to be. Even younger children in Northern Ireland sometimes describe the purpose of history in similar terms – they want to know, for example, 'how it started that there were different religions and all,' as one said.

That may seem obvious – that history can be used to explain the present – but that kind of historical understanding isn't nearly so widespread as you might think. Many people believe that the way things are today is this the way they've always been; they believe that men and women have always displayed the same gender roles as they do in contemporary Western society, that economic production has always been based on capitalist principles, that Christianity has always had the same range of beliefs and practices as today, that people of different racial backgrounds have always had the same prejudices as today. And in Northern Ireland, many people believe that the current forms of segregation, prejudice, and sectarian violence are a timeless and inevitable feature of Catholic and Protestant interaction, when in fact in many cases they're fairly recent in origin. If people think, mistakenly, that the way things are is the way they've always been, we'll have nothing to talk about in a democracy, because there's nothing to apply our judgment to. History, then, gives us something to reason about, by showing how our societal institutions have been created, and thus suggesting how they might be changed, or what steps might be necessary to preserve them.

The practical implication of this is that history education should devote attention, in part, to explaining the origin of the modern world – to helping students see how the events of the past are connected to those of the present. This isn't always the case: many of the people and events that children study have no obvious connection to contemporary issues, and their place in the curriculum seems to derive from their status as part of a traditional canon rather than from their historical importance. In the United States, for example, every child learns stories about the so-called First Thanksgiving, and about the mythical figure of Betsy Ross, who is erroneously credited with sewing the first American flag, but these stories do nothing to help them understand the modern world – or any other world, for that matter.

Perhaps a bigger problem is that students often study historical topics that are important to the modern world, but they never have a chance to explore just what the connection between past and present is, and their teachers don't explain the relevance of such topics. In Northern Ireland, for example, secondary students study topics such as Home Rule and Partition, but these are rarely presented in a context that connects them to the present – rather, they're just part of a chronological march through the past. Similarly, secondary students in the United States study topics such as Reconstruction or industrialization, which are clearly relevant to modern society, but they don't focus on that relevance, and so these fascinating topics become more seemingly trivial information to be ignored or forgotten. Teachers may understand how such events are related to the present, but students won't grasp their relevance without much more direct attention to the topic. Giving students a chance to explore the enduring legacy of historical events – their impact on the present – is a critical part of preparing them for democratic citizenship.

There's another way the connection between past and present can be obscured – one that's not as obvious, but that's just as destructive for democracy. Some approaches to history present the past as though it happened the way it *had* to happen, as though there were no alternatives open to our ancestors or, by implication, to ourselves. If history is a series of unavoidable events that leads inexorably to the present, then we're left with no room to manoeuvre. The present is simply the inevitable outcome of all that went before, and any attempt to bring about change in politics, economics, or culture is doomed to failure. And, indeed, history is sometimes used for precisely this purpose – to justify the status quo by convincing people that the way things *are* is the way they *must* be. This, of course, is antithetical to participatory democracy. Understanding how the past led to the present is useful as a basis for contemporary decision making only when it acknowledges the free will both of people in the past and of ourselves. Our ancestors made decisions in their own time that led to the governmental institutions, economic structures, or social patterns that we live with today, but they could have made other decisions, with other consequences. And if people in the past made choices that affected their future (and our present), then we too are free to make decisions that support, modify, or overturn these historical legacies. History education will support the goals of democracy, then, when it alerts students to the role of human agency and purpose in the past – and the limits to agency – so that they understand what role their own decisions might play in creating our futures.

A second way history can contribute to the humanistic goal of reasoned judgment is by giving students experience in the process of using evidence to reach conclusions. The judgments required of citizens depend, in part, on analysing evidence. People who passively accept the conclusions of others – particularly if they don't even understand the process of developing those conclusions – are liable to be manipulated in any number of ways. Those who have experience finding information, evaluating reliability, and developing interpretations – all the skills of historical inquiry – should be better able to use those skills in making decisions, and they may be more likely to recognize flaws in the conclusions of others. Just as important, students who are skilled in historical inquiry may better be able to engage with those who would use history to justify their own dominance in relations of power. This is especially important in societies, such as ours, in which access to knowledge is not always free and equal. Students who have not had such access may be better able to develop their own, convincing, historical interpretations if we give them experience in the process. This experience may help them withstand the imposition of meanings, values, and interpretations by others.

Many of the secondary students I've interviewed in Northern Ireland are particularly aware of this purpose for studying history at school. They recognize that the history they have encountered in their communities may be heavily biased, and they look to school to provide them with a wider range of facts and to expose them to multiple perspectives, so that they can, as they often tell me, make up their own minds about it. Giving students practice in making up their own minds is surely one of the noblest reasons for immersing them in the study of history, and certainly one of the ways in which history can contribute to democratic citizenship.

The implication for history education is obvious: students should engage in historical inquiry by investigating important questions and developing their own conclusions, grounded in evidence. Classrooms in which they simply absorb the conclusions already reached by others – whether historians, teachers, or textbook writers – are not likely to prepare students to engage in reasoned judgment, because they provide nothing for them to judge, nor any grounds on which to base their judgments. Indeed, scholars such as Peter Seixas have argued that expecting students to passively absorb historical information fundamentally misportrays what history is all about. Others, such as Peter Lee, note that without understanding the evidence on which historical accounts are based, we can scarcely say that a student 'knows' history at all.[3] But clearly, many classrooms don't engage students in historical inquiry; students are simply expected to learn what they're told. Again, that kind of history education might be appropriate to some kinds of political systems, but it doesn't have any clear role in contributing to citizenship in a participatory democracy.

Yet even in classrooms in which students do engage in inquiry, and where they are expected to make reasoned judgments, their experiences may not prepare them very well for citizenship. I say this because even excellent, inquiry-oriented history education too often focuses on questions, issues, or time periods that have little relevance to contemporary problems. Many history educators assume, logically enough, that if students develop the ability to use evidence to draw conclusions about historical issues, then they'll be able to apply those skills to other topics. This is a common view in both Britain and North America. A student who has compared conflicting primary source accounts of the battle at Lexington Green logically should be able to compare conflicting accounts of contemporary issues; students who have assembled evidence to answer questions about social life in the Victorian era should be able to assemble evidence to answer questions about social life today. But in fact, this may not the case. In Northern Ireland, for example, my colleague Alan McCully has noted how students can apply critical perspectives and make reasoned and reflective judgments about controversial political issues in Ireland's past, but when they are asked to apply those same abilities to parallel issues related to the current Troubles, they refuse to do so. He says that it's as though an 'emotional wall' ascends; they not only refuse to look at their own communities critically, they refuse even to accept the legitimacy of the request, as though contemporary issues should not be submitted to critical reflection.[4]

Reasoned judgment, then, may not transfer easily from one situation to another. This may seem somewhat ironic, since I've just been saying that students in Northern Ireland often think the purpose of learning history is to help them make more critical judgments about contemporary society. I would argue that this seeming contradiction arises from the fact that applying what we've learned about the past to ourselves in the present is a very difficult process, even when we know we should do it. The very difficulty of this process seems to me an argument in favour of spending more time on it in school; students aren't likely to do it very well unless they have a great deal of support and guidance in the effort. And separating school-based historical inquiry from the issues students actually care about may not be a particularly effective educational method, because it's difficult for students to make the connection between what they learn at school and what engages them outside school. If students' experiences in reasoning about evidence are meant to prepare them for the demands of citizenship, then schools may have to address historical issues that students themselves consider important, and these more frequently derive from the recent past than from more distant eras.

The first characteristic of humanistic education, then, is reasoned judgment, and I've suggested that history can contribute to this end both by giving students something to reason about and by giving them experience in the process of reaching conclusions through critical analysis of evidence. A second characteristic of humanistic education is *an expanded view of humanity.* Humanistic study can help us move beyond the belief that our own lives are the natural or universal way of being in the world, and can inspire our appreciation of the lives of those in other times and places – including those of a different ethnicity, class, gender, sexual orientation, or physical ability. This ability to recognize, respect, and even embrace the range of human diversity is critical to a pluralist democracy. We can embrace pluralism only if we truly believe that other people's views are potentially as sensible as our own – if we understand that there are reasonable ways of thinking, feeling, and believing other than those we're accustomed to.

History can help provide this expanded perspective on humanity by taking us beyond the narrow confines of our present circumstances and helping us understand the cares, the concerns, and the ways of thinking of people different from ourselves. You can hear this perspective in one of the quotes I shared at the beginning – the primary student who explained the importance of learning about people different from herself. Of course, students know that other people can be different from themselves – they know that people in the past looked, acted, and even believed differently than they do, and that the same is true for people in other parts of the world. What history can do – along with anthropology or cultural geography – is help them understand the logic of these different ways of thinking, believing, and acting. By studying the culture and the social institutions of people far removed in time and space, students can learn that there are multiple ways of being human and that their own ideas about proper social arrangements may simply be one set of practices among a range of reasonable alternatives. This recognition is absolutely critical for participatory democracy, because only when we accept that those with whom we disagree might have a reasonable basis for their beliefs can we engage in meaningful dialogue.

One implication of this for history education is obvious: students should learn about people very different from themselves, and about societies very different from their own. This may seem like a contradiction of the point I've been making about the need for more closely connecting past and present, but I believe it simply reflects the fact that history cannot be either simple or monolithic but must engage students with the past in a variety of ways. Students should explore direct connections between past and present, but they should also learn about historical topics with few such connections – Incan civilization, or Mesolithic people, or medieval heretics. It's precisely because these people seem so different from us that they are worth learning more about, so that we can broaden our perspectives and, hopefully, learn to appreciate the diversity of humanity. In the United States, this would mean studying a wider range of topics than is the norm. Currently, our history curriculum focuses almost entirely on national history – in other words, on those people most likely to be similar to the students themselves. But by studying the social institutions and cultures of people far removed in time and space, students should be better able to understand the multiple ways of being human. They might be better prepared for pluralist democracy if they had a chance to examine more closely the lives of people who have not traditionally been part of their own national story.

A second implication is that, whatever the topic or time period being covered, students should be exposed to a variety of viewpoints of people involved in the events of the day, so that they understand that differing opinions are a normal and natural part of social interaction. In a sense, this is hardly a controversial conclusion, because any historian recognizes that there was a diversity of beliefs, practices, and perspectives at any given time in history. But this isn't always part of history education: very often, the complexity of the past is simplified to such an extent that students are presented with an utterly false portrait of history, usually one of happy consensus. U.S. students, for example, rarely learn that a large portion of the colonial population opposed the American Revolution, much less that there were significant controversies within Britain over the nature and extent of parliamentary representation. Instead, they're presented with a picture in which all colonists were on one side, and all the British on the other. They're even less likely to learn that many Americans opposed the Vietnam War, unless they've seen it in the movie *Forrest Gump*. If students think everyone in a given country or community agreed on such issues, they'll have few resources for understanding why people might disagree today, and they'll have little reason to take other people's ideas seriously. Again, learning about different opinions in history doesn't *guarantee* that students will accept such differences today, but it helps to create the conditions under which such acceptance might seem reasonable to them.

This openness to difference brings us to the third and final characteristic of humanistic education – *experience in public deliberation*. This aspect of humanistic education unifies and brings meaning to the first two, and of course it's practically synonymous with one of the defining characteristics of participatory democracy. It's not enough simply to be able to reason carefully or to recognize the humanity of others. Humanistic study draws on these two capacities to bring people together – to engage them in discussion, where they reason together to make judgments; and, if we take democratic citizenship seriously, these must be judgments that sustain the common good or lead to social justice. This is the perspective you hear in the third quote I shared with you at the beginning, when Daniel said, 'You can learn to ... be more appreciative of what people think and what they believe in, because it doesn't help you if you just believe one thing and think everyone else is wrong.'

This may be the trickiest part of history education, the purpose that is the least obvious and the most subject to manipulation. We certainly can't count on history to *produce* a concern with the common good or to *guarantee* that students will be willing to take part in collaborative judgments with others. We can, however, make sure that they have the *chance to consider* the common good, and the *opportunity to reason together* with others. There are far more historical topics than we could ever cover in schools. When we make choices about which to include in the curriculum, then, one of our criteria should be the extent to which given topics promote consideration of the common good. Students should be exposed to those historical topics that force them to consider issues of justice – the impact of racism, for example, or gender roles, dictatorship, warfare, colonialism, economic relations, and so on. Again, there is no neutral or objective basis for making curricular choices – these choices will based on some criteria, and if we want to promote citizenship, we'd be better served by making these choices because of their ability to call attention to issues of social justice rather than on the basis of convenience or tradition. Students will be better prepared for democracy if they learn about the labour movement rather than early explorers of the Mississippi River; they'll be better prepared for democracy if they learn about imperialism rather than Betsy Ross.

In addition, students should have the chance to publicly discuss the justice of past events or social arrangements, and the justice of their legacy. Some teachers, and some historians, claim that students *shouldn't* judge what happened in the past – that this isn't what 'real history' is. That's nonsense. We all reach judgments about history, all the time. The Holocaust, slavery, suffrage, the Vietnam War, the civil rights movement, the Crusades, the end of apartheid, the Ku Klux Klan, the bombing of Hiroshima, September 11 – surely all of us have made judgments about whether these contributed to or detracted from the common good. Children certainly have; in my interviews with them, they consistently point to issues of justice (or 'fairness,' as they usually call it) as one of the principal reasons for their interest in the subject. They want to know about slavery and racial discrimination, they want to know about restrictions on women's roles in society, they want to know about conflicts between Europeans and Native Americans, and they want to know about the Holocaust. These topics interest them because they involve issues of justice or fairness, and this interest might well motivate them to study any number of historical topics. Students are going to judge the events of the past, whether we ask them to or not; the question for educators is how best to use public deliberation to help students make judgments that are informed, reasonable, and publicly justifiable. Maybe it's possible to study historical topics involving oppression or subjugation without making judgments; maybe there's even a place for that kind of history in the halls of academia. But I don't see any role for it when we're trying to prepare students for democracy. Omitting discussion of justice from history classrooms would be an outrageously missed opportunity.

But engaging students in discussions of fairness or justice is not the same as leading them to predetermined conclusions about what should have taken place in the past or what should be done today. The purpose of deliberation is to enable students to work with others to reach such conclusions jointly, not to reproduce the beliefs of teachers, textbooks, historians, or politicians. The great danger of history that focuses on questions of the common good is that those in positions of authority may think that they already know what the common good is, and that their role is to reproduce their own opinions in students – to tell them what they're supposed to think about Vietnam or Reagan or the Gulf War. We hear a lot of this in the United States right now – that schools should be teaching more history and more civics so that everyone will support the government. That makes me shudder, of course. But just as disturbing is when colleagues with whom I agree politically suggest that schools should exist to turn students into miniature versions of themselves – little leftists, usually. In a pluralist democracy, we cannot impose any single vision of the common good on students, or teach them any single set of judgments about history. But in a deliberative democracy, we can engage them in discussions in which they work together to develop their own judgments and their own visions.

Let me close with another extract from an interview with children in the United States and a brief story about history teaching. When I interviewed Kathy and Curtis, who were about eleven years, I asked them why it would be important to know about various topics in history. One of the events they brought up was the U.S. civil rights movement, which they had studied earlier in the year at school and which they had told me they thought was one of the most important events in history.

CURTIS:	Like that [1950s segregation], it looks like everybody's looking at the African American, like he's real bad and stuff, and they don't like him, it looks like.
KATHY:	Learn how they were always mean.
CURTIS:	How they were treated and stuff.
INTERVIEWER:	Well, why would it be important to study about that?
KATHY:	Because we don't want to treat black people like that today, and if we know that –
CURTIS:	If someone treated him like that, they'll probably arrest him and stuff –
INTERVIEWER:	That's a good point. Do you think knowing about history would –

CURTIS: Change your mind or something?
INTERVIEWER: Yeah.
KATHY: Well, yeah, because if I didn't know that there was like a war, kind of like, having black people, maybe I would be really mean to black people.
CURTIS   And didn't know that immigrants came, you would probably treat the immigrants mean and stuff because they were from another country and talk another language.
KATHY: And if I didn't really know about Martin Luther King and all that, then it would be like, 'Oh, it's just a man who did this, doesn't really matter,' or something like that.

These students clearly expected history to have a purpose. They weren't interested in studying it 'for its own sake' but because of the insight it gave them into issues of justice, human relations, and the shape of modern society. Perhaps most important, they expected history to help them explore the moral foundations of their own behaviour in the present: they assumed that learning about civil rights, or the treatment of immigrants, in historical contexts would help them understand how to approach such topics today, and that that's why these were subjects in school.

But now let me relate a somewhat different story. A few years ago I was in a seminar that was composed mainly of doctoral students in history, although there was one high school history teacher in the group. She taught in inner-city Louisville, Kentucky, in a school in which nearly all students were African American. The discussion in the class turned to how representations of slavery in the public school curriculum have changed over the years. Since none of these doctoral students really knew anything about teaching, they turned to the teacher and asked whether in her school they approached slavery as a topic with enduring relevance. She said they try not to; she said that sometimes students at her school try to bring up the connection between past and present but that the teachers always put a stop to it, because modern race relations don't have anything to do with what they're supposed to be studying in history, and it just gets the students agitated. She was proud that she and her colleagues never let students get them off the official curriculum and onto 'all these things that aren't really relevant' – such as race relations.

I wish I could tell myself that this is an isolated example. Unfortunately, I know it's not. There are entire school districts where the topic of slavery has been prohibited from history classrooms. Too many educators, in the United States and elsewhere, go out of their way to avoid addressing the relevance of history, either because they believe that history shouldn't be relevant, or because they don't understand its relevance, or most disturbingly because they recognize all too well how relevant history is, and they're unwilling to open doors that might allow students to draw their own conclusions, conclusions that might challenge the status quo. The last thing these schools want is for students to get agitated about history.

We all make commitments when we study history, or when we teach it. The teacher from Louisville was committed to preventing her students from understanding their own past and from making judgments about current social arrangements. Kathy and Curtis, on the other hand, were committed to using history to explore their obligations to those who are different from themselves. It's obvious which set of commitments I prefer. If history is to prepare students for participatory democracy, then Kathy and Curtis's understanding of the topic is far more meaningful than that of the teacher who didn't want her African-American students to discuss race relations. History deserves a place in public education only if we can develop a meaningful and publicly articulated rationale for it, one rooted in pluralism, participation, and deliberation.

NOTES

1 Most of these ideas have been developed in close collaboration with Linda S. Levstik. See Keith C. Barton and Linda S. Levstik, *Teaching History for the Common Good* (Mahwah, NJ: Lawrence Erlbaum Associates, 2004), and Linda S. Levstik and Keith C. Barton, 'Committing Acts of History: Mediated Action, Humanistic Education, and Participatory Democracy,' in William Stanley, ed., *Critical Issues in Social Studies Research for the 21st Century* (Greenwich, CT: Information Age Publishing, 2001), 119–48.
2 Elliot Eisner, 'Can the Humanities Be Taught in American Public Schools?' in B. Ladner, ed., *The Humanities in Precollegiate Education*, Eighty-third Yearbook of the National Society for the Study of Education, Part II (Chicago: University of Chicago Press, 1984), 115; Benjamin Barber, *Strong*

Democracy: Participatory Politics for a New Age (Berkeley: University of California Press, 1984), 138.

3 Peter Seixas, 'The Community of Inquiry as a Basis for Knowledge and Learning: The Case of History,' *American Educational Research Journal* 30 (Summer 1993): 305–24; Peter Lee, 'Historical Knowledge and the National Curriculum,' in Richard Aldrich, ed. *History in the National Curriculum* (London: Kogan Page, 1991), 48.

4 Keith C. Barton and Alan W. McCully, 'History Teaching and the Perpetuation of Memories: The Northern Ireland Experience,' in Edward Cairns and Micheal Roe, eds., *The Role of Memories in Ethnic Conflict* (New York: Palgrave, Macmillan, 2003), 105–24.

5 Remembering Our Past: An Examination of the Historical Memory of Young Québécois

JOCELYN LÉTOURNEAU

It is usually thought that young people, for different reasons, know very little about history. Bodies like the Dominion Institute of Canada, for instance, have commissioned multiple polls over time to show that, when questioned about features of the past, young people, mostly students, would be unable to answer correctly more than two or three times out of ten.[1] In Quebec as well, we find numerous studies showing the lack of empirical knowledge among young people about the history of the province or of the nation – whatever you choose to call it. Summing up this catastrophic state of affairs, one publication was even titled *Trou de mémoire*.[2]

My feeling is that we must be careful about polls that try to measure the level of empirical knowledge possessed by students. In that game, even professional historians may lose their shirts, their skirts, or, worse, their reputation. Personally, I'd be afraid to be tested in a poll. I'm sure I would perform badly! Does this mean I'm without a knowledge or even impressions of the past? Not at all. It is the same with young people. When, instead of testing them about specific details of the past, you ask such putative 'green minds' to account for the history of Quebec, you find that they know quite a lot of things. You also find that they can account for the history of Quebec in a pretty coherent manner. This account may be not as sophisticated as yours and mine. But still, we are far from a *trou de mémoire,* and far also from a confused or senseless account of the past.

In this chapter I will present the preliminary results of research I did on young people aged fifteen to twenty-five, research that dealt with their general knowledge and sense of the representation of the historical experience of Quebec.[3] My concern was to get into the historical memory of young people in Quebec, memory that I consider to be a kind of engine of their historical consciousness.

Although this chapter is focused on the case of Quebec, I think research such as mine could be replicated anywhere in the country, and I hope such research will be done in the near future.[4] The significance of such research is multifaceted and profound. Indeed, a number of central theoretical as well as practical educational issues can be raised or addressed from the perspective of such research. The acquisition of historical knowledge in children and adolescents is certainly one such issue. We know that children and adolescents are not unaware of representations of the past, that they know many things about life in different times. We also know that they get most of their knowledge outside the classroom. How are representations of the past being created in children's minds? How do children come to get trapped in these meta-representations, or general frameworks, that will act for them as sorts of intellectual crutches that help them understand the world in its past and present, and to anticipate its future as well? How does information of different types mix in a person's mind to produce ways of seeing that, over time, will consolidate in 'mythistories' that may undermine his or her capacity to see the world another way?

In Canada, though it is true all over the planet, we know that the existence of such mythistories looms over the future of the country. Indeed, because of those mythistories, Québécois see English Canadians in a certain and peculiar way, while Québécois are seen by English Canadians in another way, which is just as peculiar. It is the same with francophones and anglophones, Easterners and Westerners, people living in big cities and those living outside those pockets, the Northerners and Southerners, and so on. To understand the way mythistories shape the historical mind of children – children who become adults who do not revise most, or at least some, of their basic references – is certainly a challenge in today's research.

Another topic of prime importance raised by research such as mine relates to the consequences of education. Indeed, if we consider mythistories as a constraint on seeing things in different ways, if not actually preventing a fresh future from unfolding, how is it possible to get away from these mythistories? Is education the best possible way to achieve such a goal? If so, then, how should we proceed in order to deconstruct mythistories? Just by giving young people more information so they become concerned people? I have serious doubts about that. Education, yes. But how can we really open children to new stories that will make them see the world, and other cultures as well, from a different point of view? We haven't yet come to a consensus about these issues. More research needs to be done. Mine is a modest contribution in that direction.

This chapter will be divided into three parts. First, I provide the results of my research. Basically, I will explore what young Québécois know about the historical experience of Quebec and how they account for that experience. That narrative, as you will see, is indeed interesting in its structure and content. When accounting for the historical experience of Quebec, practically all students I tested, from Grade 11 to the university level, used a narrative that is, in a way, traditional. It refers to the timeless quest of Québécois, poor alienated people, for emancipation from their oppressors.

The persistence of such a narrative in young people's minds is indeed amazing, for it fits poorly with what professional historians have been saying for the past twenty-five years. The persistence of that narrative is also amazing because it is at odds with the current situation of Quebec, at least from an economic point of view. So this question: Why is *this* narrative, instead of any other narrative, being used, adopted, recounted by the students? An exploration of this question constitutes the second part of this chapter.

Finally, I will focus on the following question: If we find the students' narrative unsatisfactory for scientific and political reasons, then how can we take the students away from it and offer them an alternative narrative that would meet the requirements of historians' practice and would also be challenging for the future of Canada-Quebec? In other words, can we get away from a narrative that is at the heart of a collective identity? And, if so, how can we do it?

What Do Young People Know about Quebec's Past?

Before going any further with my initial question – 'What do young people know about Quebec's past?' – I must point out two things related to the methodology of my research. I mentioned earlier that I was dissatisfied with polls that give us a lot of quantitative data but very few insight into historical memory. To avoid the limits and the deficiencies of polls, I decided to use a more qualitative process. I asked young people to write short essays of about two or three pages. The initial stimulus I gave them to start writing took the form of a question – in French: *Présentez ou racontez, comme vous la percevez, la savez ou vous*

vous en souvenez, l'histoire du Québec depuis le début; in English: Please account for the history of Quebec since the beginning, the way you see it, remember it, or understand it.

After giving the students about forty-five minutes to write down their response, I collected all the essays in the classrooms. Students were not notified in advance they would be tested in this way, so they could not prepare for it. They were told that the test was being carried out for academic research. They were asked not to identify themselves on the sheets of paper, so I have reason to think that much of the stress they might have felt during the event was eliminated. The students were of course told there were no good nor bad answers, but I also asked them to think about addressing the question as seriously as possible.

Overall, 403 students fulfilled the task. Out of that number, 237 essays came from university students, 53 from Grade 11 students, 51 from students in the final year of secondary schools, and 104 from students attending CEGEPS – Quebec's junior colleges. Although this number may not be large, it is enough to support my conclusions, given the repetitive character of the narrative I found in the essays.

The second point I want to stress before going on with the question of the young people's narrative of the past is the following. The research was undertaken in the Quebec City region. As is well known, most people living in this area are from a French-Canadian cultural background. As a matter of fact, more than 98 per cent of the students we tested were from that cultural background, even those who attended an anglophone CEGEP. For that reason, we cannot pretend that the results of the research can be extended in the same way to all young Québécois. For example, Québécois with English-Canadian backgrounds would probably account for the historical experience of Quebec in a different manner than that found in this study. I have no idea whatsoever how Québécois from other cultural backgrounds, or newcomers to the province, would account for its historical experience. That is a fantastic field of research into which I will venture in the near future.[5] Yet, my feeling is that people who have been socialized in a cultural milieu, within the parameters of a culture with a strong institutional coherence, will share a set of references, including an account of the past. My guess is that, if I had done my research in the Montreal area, a region characterized by more cultural diversity, young Québécois with a French-Canadian background would probably have accounted for the historical experience of Quebec in the same manner as those in the Quebec City area.

Now let's get to the first question: How do young Québécois with a French-Canadian historical background account for the history of Quebec? First, their narrative is highly linear. Progression, regression, digression, continuity, and rupture, more than paradox, dissonance, ambiguity, or ambivalence, are the basic narrative structures of their story. Students' accounts of the history of Quebec also revolve around a set of characters and events that inhabits a great canon of historical actions. Those characters and actions are bound together in a general plot that intersects with the classical nationalist narrative of Quebec's historical experience.

This is not the place to go into the intricate details of that narrative. I will provide only the general features of the story.

1. Mostly, students' accounts begin with the coming of the French into the St Lawrence valley. Aboriginal people are around, but the course of events is being driven by the Europeans.
2. The central event in the history of Quebec is the Conquest of New France by the British in 1759. From then on, the historical experience of Quebec is, according to students, nothing but the expression of a conflict between archetypal francophones and anglophones.
3. Among the events mentioned most frequently by students, we find the Quebec Act of 1774, the Rebellions of 1837–8, Confederation, the First and Second World Wars, October 1970, and the two referendums in 1980 and 1995.
4. Characters such as Papineau and Durham (a figure much detested by young Québécois) are cast the frame of the enduring conflict between the French and the English.
5. Among the most frequently mentioned and most appreciated figures in students story, we find Jacques Cartier, Samuel de Champlain, and René Lévesque.
6. Pierre Trudeau, a central icon in anglophone Canada, especially in Ontario, does not attract a great deal of interest from these young people, even though this research was done a short time after he passed away.
7. Last but not least, women, Aboriginal people, and immigrants are secondary characters in young people's story of Quebec.

Overall, the students' narrative follows a framework that is very coherent, logical, and strong, and that develops in this way:

- Chapter 1, New France: This period is a time of goodness, an age of innocence. It is possible to live in French. There are some problems, of course, but the problem of fighting for cultural and linguistic survival does not occur. (If I may introduce a side idea here, it is clear that, saying this, students are making an anachronistic statement, for there is no struggle for linguistic survival at this time. We must remember that they are looking at the past from the other end of the telescope, the present being in a direct relation with the past.)
- Chapter 2, The Conquest: This event marks the great fall of the French in North America. It is a dramatic rupture that opens the door for a decline, a regression of the French. The historical experience of Quebec afterward is a continuous struggle for power between the English and the French, the will of the former being to dominate, through varying levels of coercion, the latter.
- Chapter 3, The Quiet Revolution: This event, which occurs in the 1960s, marks the beginning of a new era, a reversal of the previous situation. It is a time of great awakening for the French, who reject many features of their traditional identity, namely agriculturalism, messianism, and anti-democratism. The Quiet Revolution is a moment of historical liberation. René Lévesque, more than Jean Lesage, is the leader of this renaissance.
- Chapter 4, Today: Unfortunately, the momentum of the Quiet Revolution seems to be lost in the present time. Since the last referendum (1995), Quebec has entered a period of indecision, not to say of stalling. It is with this nostalgic and melancholic observation that the students' account of the historical experience of Quebec comes to its conclusion.

Some of you may find this narrative disappointing and, depending on your political point of view, call it too simple, too biased, or too focused. Such a reaction may be expected, but it is useless. The task is not to blame the students for excessive simplicity or to look for a scapegoat, but to understand why the students accounted for the historical experience of Quebec in *that* way rather than in any other way.

Why *That* Narrative?

Many hypotheses come to mind to explain the formation of the narrative.

The Curriculum and Textbooks

The first and probably the easiest hypothesis is that the students' narra-tive, influenced by the compulsory 'Quebec and Canada' history course they take in Grade 11, is an over-simplification of the narrative found in textbooks used in the classroom, textbooks that reflect the orientation of the program of history implemented by Quebec's Ministry of Educa-tion about twenty years ago.[6]

   This hypothesis has been put forward by different scholars. Although we find some truth in it, I think it is not the most accurate hypothesis to explain the students' beliefs, for the content of the textbooks is not a digest of the nationalist view of Quebec's historical experience. In the mid-nineties I personally made a review of the textbooks accepted by the Ministry of Education and used in class.[7] It is an exaggeration to say that the point of view expressed in those textbooks is narrowly nation-alistic. The francophones are not represented merely as the passive victims of the anglophones. Nor are they considered as perennial losers. Their patriotism is oriented not only towards Quebec but also towards Canada (or towards a certain idea of Canada). Most important, per-haps, the general representation of the historical experience of Quebec presented in these textbooks is more optimistic than pessimistic. The material condition of Quebeckers is certainly not reduced to the arche-type of the Poor, the Insignificant, and the Victim. The ideas of a priest-ridden society and a surviving nation are not basic representations upon which the textbooks' narrative is built. Rather, they depict Quebec society as an open place, absorbing innovations at a fast rate and developing quickly as a market-oriented society. In other words, Que-bec is equated with the changes in the continental and Atlantic worlds. Textbooks, in other words, are very far from what students insisted upon in their accounts.

   Neither is the Quebec Ministry of Education curriculum for the his-tory of Canada-Quebec oriented towards narrowly nationalist goals. Indeed, if one accepts that the general aim of this course is to give students the means to know more about the historical experience of Quebec within its multiple contexts, then we have to say that the curriculum is quite acceptable. Yet, it is important to insist on two points. First, the program implemented by the ministry,[8] and which is currently under revision, includes different targets ('objectifs terminaux') among which we find: 1) the understanding of the Conquest, its causes and its effects; 2) the description of the events of 1837–8 and the establishment of the Union of the two Canadas; 3) the analysis of the Duplessis era from the point of view of an opposition between traditionalism and modernization; and, 4) the characterization of the Quiet Revolution and its aftermath. Clearly, there are possible interminglings between certain objectives of the program and the themes in the students' narratives. In other words, students' accounts are structured partly according to the orientation of the program. But I must be clear on this: we cannot pretend that the program, which is comprehensive rather than politically oriented, and which is after all based on brute facts of the past (no one can deny 1759 or 1837–8), explicitly or in a direct way nourishes students' narrative.

Second, the content of the textbooks is more subtle than narrowly focused. That said, it is possible to find in their content brute facts that will sustain a nationalist narrative of the historical experience of Quebec. Yet, this content does not by itself lead a student to view the historical experience of Quebec as something that is dramatic and whose central dynamic is the tribulations of a kind of unrealized historical Subject, or *sujet manqué* – the Québécois.

To sum up, both the ministry's program and textbooks can sustain many accounts of the historical experience of Quebec. Their aims and content are largely reasonable and acceptable. It is certainly possible to improve them, and the Working Committee on the teaching of history, chaired by Jacques Lacoursière ten years ago, has made several recommendations to do so.[9] But basically, it is untrue to say that the ministry's program and textbooks belong to some sort of patriotic enterprise designed to shape the student's mind in a narrow way. We ought to explore another hypothesis to understand why, among all possible narratives, students kept using one in particular.

The 'System of the Classroom'

I'd now like to turn to an examination of the 'system of the classroom.' My feeling, and this has been documented by some studies, is that teachers, who hold a prominent place in the system of the classroom, are very much responsible for the structuring and maintenance of the specific account students have of the historical experience of Quebec.[10] Why is this so? There are many reasons. One lies in the fact that many history teachers were trained a long time ago – that is, at a time when the historiographical paradigm set out by Séguin, Brunet, and Frégault was dominant. Although contested by research done in the 1980s and

1990s, that paradigm, which insists on the victimization of francophones in Canada, remains strong in the mind of many teachers. As everyone knows, it is not easy to abandon a paradigm and to opt for another.

A second reason is linked to the limited training many teachers have received. Some of them, as is widely known, do not have specialized training in history. Their knowledge of history consists of a more or less superficial vision of that which has been. Most of the time, that vision is articulated around the major political events in the history of Canada and Quebec. Of course, those teachers want to give their students the best information possible. To compensate for their lack of information, they rely on textbooks. What they find in textbooks, however, is in accordance with their own basic knowledge of the history of the country. They may certainly read the whole text, but what remains after the reading is that information and data that reinforce their basic understanding of the history of Canada-Quebec. This is possible because, as I noted above, one can find in these textbooks content that will support a nationalist history of Quebec. And one has to admit that the historical experience of Canada-Quebec can sustain such an account of that which has been. That such an account is, or is not, the most accurate or appropriate account of the history of Canada-Quebec is another question – a question that many teachers cannot even raise because they are not in a position to think of another possible narrative to explain the historical experience of Quebec.

A third reason why we can hold the teachers largely responsible for the presence of the narrative I found in students' essays is that teachers may find it is easiest to transmit this 'traditional' account of the history of Quebec as the *best* general representation of Quebec's historical experience.

And this brings me to one of the major points of my argument. It is my assumption that when students get to Grade 11 – that is, at the time when they are being taught their first systematic course of Canada-Quebec history – they are not empty vessels. They already have a sort of vision of the historical experience of Quebec. That historical vision is certainly, in most cases, very simplistic. It has formed over time, nourished by many sources. It is articulated around basic narrative structures among which we find the binary notions of Canada and Quebec, anglophones and francophones, federalism and nationalism. I'm not saying that students have a deep knowledge of, or can rightly contextualize, these notions to which they refer. The contrary is probably true in most of the cases. What I want to stress is that those basic narrative structures, and the binary notions that are at their core, act as a sort of basic matrix of understanding, a simple way of comprehending the complexity of the past (and the present as well).

In other words, by the time they get to Grade 11, students are already in a position to understand the past in a *specific way* and not in all possible ways. They are already caught up in the canonical categories of understanding that make a culture a culture. Students are already trapped, most of the time unconsciously, within the limits of a thinkable history of Quebec. And of course, when we speak of a thinkable history of Quebec, we ought to speak, as well, of an unthinkable history of Quebec.

Before going any further, I must add that these observations about students in Quebec with a French-Canadian cultural heritage are also applicable elsewhere in Canada, to people of other cultural backgrounds. In a remarkable book, Daniel Francis has convincingly demonstrated that English Canada, as an imagined community, was very much dependent on some basic mythistories that strengthened the historical consciousness of a particular community of communication and reference.[11] Things have not changed much. It is clear that, even today, most anglophone Canadians are trapped in a canon that makes them see Canada – and Quebec, of course – through a series of references or canonical figures that sometimes narrowly coincides with what Canada or Quebec was or actually is. To take on the title of an article I once published in the *Globe and Mail*, we are all trapped by mistaken identities.[12]

To return to my previous point about the thinkable/unthinkable history of Quebec, let's imagine a situation in which a teacher, with little training in history, faces a class composed of students who have only a very basic idea of the historical experience of Quebec. The chances are great that the teacher and students will implicitly agree about a representation of the past because they belong to the same culture. The same will, of course, happen when the teacher *does* have training in the history of Quebec but thinks that the unfortunate and unhappy history of Quebec is the best possible account of the historical experience of this collectivity, a situation that is not at all uncommon.

What if a teacher and a group of students do not belong to the same culture? I don't have data to support a hypothesis about that question. My guess is that confusion may arise in students' minds. It is also possible that students might lose interest in their history class because the account that is being taught to them is useless, incomprehensible, or meaningless. In any case, I think that a historical account being taught in class will matter in students' minds if it is reinforced by other accounts outside the class. As we know, the history class is not the only source of historical information students get. Television, movies, museums, family discussions, non-fiction books and novels, newspapers and magazines are probably more important in the shaping of their historical minds. If the teacher says something that is not reinforced by other information outside the class, or something that does not belong to a dominant common way of seeing, then it might well be cast aside. It is not easy to go against the public discourse around which a community of communication structures its identity.

Collective Memory

The last point leads me to a third hypothesis I formulated to understand the particular narrative I found in students' essays. That hypothesis holds that the presence of a historical collective memory is an important factor in shaping students' narratives about the historical experience of Quebec. This hypothesis is not really original. Yet, very few studies have been done to understand the process by which a historical collective memory circulating in a society would be grasped by people living in that society. I'll come back to this point later.

For now, I would like to point out that the existence of a historical collective memory specific to the Franco-Québécois with a French-Canadian background is something that is well known and has been documented at length. Historical collective memory may be defined as a set of references including, among others, teleological schemes, clichés, stereotypes, ideas, representations of all sorts, reified characters, fragments *of énoncés* – all items through which the past, the present, and the future are not only decoded and constructed, but also anticipated. A historical collective memory is (probably) inevitably founded on mythistories. Rather than bemoaning this circumstance, the challenge is to try to find the means to deconstruct historical collective memory, so a space can be created in which new references can come and grow. In the end, another historical collective memory, hopefully more sensitive to the complexity of the past, may emerge.

In Quebec, at the present time, the historical collective memory that remains dominant in the ideological world of the Franco-Québécois, and that I found in students' accounts, displeases many people for different reasons. Some of them find this historical collective memory inaccurate with regard to the need to build up new common ground, a consensus in Quebec, so all the Québécois can re-create their identity as a *nation québécoise*. Those people, among whom we find some of the finest intellectuals in today's Quebec, are claiming a new memory and a new history for the Québécois.[13] As far as I'm concerned, I welcome such a project of remaking a collective memory and history: I made a plea for it in one of my last books.[14]

The difficulty I have with the way the project has been conducted so far is that it is driven by a specific political agenda, that of the building of a new Quebec nation. Personally, I'd rather get into the business of revising the collective memory and history with the aim of restoring the idea of *canadianité,* which refers to the acceptance of dissonance as being at the core of the historical experience of the country. I consider *canadianité* to be quite different from *canadienneté,* which is nothing but the central concept supporting and legitimizing Canada's nation-rebuilding process, a process that may be criticized as much as that of Quebec. I wonder sometimes if the concept of nation, which is like a siren's song for people governing in both Quebec City and Ottawa, has not become a constraint rather than a force to open up a future for the country.

I return here to my main argument, that students' narratives reflect a historical collective memory, that of the Franco-Québécois of French-Canadian heritage. While this can be easily demonstrated, it is more challenging, especially in regard to the task of the historical education we should give to young people, to understand how a historical collective memory becomes the vision of young people. In other words, how does the historical collective memory penetrate the individual mind?

I see this process of articulation that way. (Please note that my argument is appropriate with regard to the students I tested. I don't pretend here to elaborate any general theory on the making of historical consciousness regardless of space, time, and culture.)

First, let me make a point we often forget: children are intelligent and wise, and their minds are very much open to information. They learn and absorb a lot of information, even though we may think they don't. On this basis, I assume that, during their childhood, including the time they were in primary school, the students I tested were given – and got for themselves – a lot of information about the history of Canada, of Quebec, and of the world. This information was of different types and was more or less reliable. It came from several sources: family, movies, television series, school, friends, politicians, cartoons, and so on. This information nourished, in the children's minds, an elementary, very rudimentary vision of that which has been in regard to Canada, Quebec, and the world. I also assume that this information was quickly organized into metaphorical structures. It is at this stage that the very general idea of the good Franco and the bad Anglo, for instance, probably took form. I'm not saying that this particular idea was being conveyed to the children in such a direct or narrow way. But such an idea, which circulates around, especially in the discourse of politicians and in the press, and which, for young minds, is a simple and efficient means to understand the complexity of the world, becomes an important tool for understanding the dynamics of the country.

Second, what we should understand is that this first, and often highly simplistic, vision becomes the nexus around which orbits a lot of information in students' minds. Through this process, a basic matrix of understanding is rapidly structured. Such a matrix acts more or less like a large planet that absorbs everything that comes into its gravitational field. In such a scheme, in-coming information is either absorbed or rejected. Information that is not compatible with this system of understanding is deflected or turned away. In that regard, we may say that this basic matrix of understanding opens the way for the making of the thinkable and the unthinkable. By unthinkable, I don't mean something that does not exist. I mean something that is not – or cannot be – conceptualized in a system of understanding.

Third, by the time young people enter Grade 11, they possess, in a more or less sophisticated form, a basic matrix of understanding with which they decode and encode the world around them and the information that comes to them or that they get by themselves. Surely, young people may be open to a more complex process of understanding. Most of the time, however, this process involves a simple expansion of the existing matrix of understanding and not a change to its fundamental structure. To get away from that basic matrix of understanding would demand nothing short of a massive intervention that would break the primitive nexus around which it is structured. So even though young people are being taught information that could lead to the formation of, let's say, a new representation of the historical experience of Quebec, it is unlikely that this will happen. They would rather stick with the basic matrix of understanding they already possess. They can easily defend their interpretation because they can find, in teachers' lectures, a lot of information that is compatible with that matrix. They can also find, in Quebec's past, a confirmation of their understanding of the historical experience of Quebec. Although seeing the history of Quebec through the prism of the conflict between the good Franco and the bad Anglo is as simple as picturing the French Québécois as the black sheep of Canada, one cannot deny the existence, over a long period of time, of asymmetrical relations of power between the two solitudes in this country. Nor can one deny that the way Québécois act within Confederation may displease many Canadians. This is stuff that consolidates the basic matrix of understanding and mythistories that structure the way young people – and others – see the past, understand the present, and anticipate the future. This is, in other words, how they build their historical consciousness.

Fourth, after Grade 11, as we know, very few Québécois take any further courses in history. One can conclude that the great majority of young Québécois will stick to their basic matrix of understanding, which will expand or wrinkle but not change in fundamentals. This conclusion is documented by my data, which show no structural modification in the accounts made by university students from those by students in Grade 11. Although this fact may be unfortunate, it reflects how difficult it is to modify a structure of understanding that is so dominant and pervasive.

Can We Abandon or Replace a Historical Narrative?

Does this conclusion mean there is no hope of changing the situation, that it is impossible to modify a structure of understanding? Does it mean that, as educators, we have no room to act and that our fine research is, in the end, unable to transform anything? I answer no to these questions, but we have to face the situation realistically. When thinking about modifying the historical account of Quebec's past being proposed by the Franco-Québécois with a French-Canadian background, it is hopeless to think of change in the short run. I have discussed above the extent to which the system within the classroom, on the one hand, and the existence of a collective historical memory, on the other, together reinforce a vision of the past that is at the core of a collective identity. To unbuild a historical system of representation – whether in Quebec, Canada, or elsewhere in the world – is not a simple task. In these matters, patience is of prime importance. That doesn't mean we should not initiate remedies. What can we do?

First, we should stop considering young people as empty vessels. By themselves, outside the classroom and in their social lives, they acquire a vision of the past that may be simple and simplistic but that is coherent and strong. Perhaps teachers should start by recognizing the vision that students already have. Instead of immediately transmitting information, teachers could try, first, to enter the students' basic matrix of understanding in order to explore its limitations. Teachers could then try to give students the means to construct a different pattern of understanding that would be a more reliable reflection of the complexity of the past. Such a pattern of understanding would also give the students the feeling that the past is an open process of evolution, a process free of teleology, a process that does not obey any simple logic, a process that cannot be reduced to the struggle between good and evil. This approach may inspire in students a sense of historical empathy as well as a sense of history – two qualities needed to help young people develop into responsible, reflective persons and critical citizens.

I also think – although I acknowledge that this is a personal utopia – that we should try to consider and to structure the historical experience of Canada-Quebec within a new general metaphor.[15] To repeat, in my mind, only a new metaphor can replace an old one. If we consider that metaphors like the one of the good Francos and the bad Anglos, or the one that says Canada has, from the beginning, developed as the best country in the world, or the one that considers the country as forming one nation from coast to coast – if we consider that metaphors like these and many others are unsatisfactory, then we have to look for something else. What are the metaphors that would allow us to rethink the whole experience of the country in a way that is accurate from an evidence-based and a political point of view? I think that the metaphor of dissonance, embedded in the concept of *canadianité,* has some interest in that regard. This metaphor avoids the limits and the deficiencies of the 'all-Canadian' thesis and the 'limited identities' thesis. Of course, the metaphor of dissonance does not fit well within the symbolic process of nation building into which Canada and Quebec have entered, on a sort of competitive basis, over the last thirty years. Personally, I'm not disturbed by such incompatibility. I propose to reread the historical and the actual course of the country. I have a crystal clear representation of who I am: I practise evidence-based history; I do not adhere to partisan politics!

Even though the metaphor of dissonance would not be considered useful by those who teach the history of Canada-Quebec in the classroom, I think that we must avoid leaving young people in a sort of vacuum regarding the representation of the country. To deconstruct visions or metaphors we find unsatisfactory is only half the duty of teaching. We must also offer an alternative view of things – a view that is coherent and strong. If we are fair enough to say that this alternative representation is not a definitive one, in no way must we tell students that all representations are equally valuable. We know that there are representations that are more accurate than others. Certainly, it might be the duty of the teacher to introduce students to different representations of the past. But the teacher must not leave students in a babel of interpretation and competitive stories that confuses young people rather than liberating them from a former limited way of thinking. Deliberation, we ought to remember, is at the beginning and at the end of the historical endeavour.

Overall, and this is going to be my last point, the teacher is at the heart of any qualitative transformation in the collective historical consciousness of students. For that reason, as the Lacoursière Committee has stated, we should not spare efforts to improve the training of those who will bring young people into one of their most systematic and lasting adventures in the past of Canada-Quebec. Nevertheless, we must not expect this transformation to emerge because of the quality of the teaching alone. This transformation will occur when a new, original synthesis of the historical experience of Quebec is produced, a synthesis that has broad influence all through the society. Such a synthesis might take the form of a movie, a television program, a book, or a symposium. Many possibilities and combinations are open here. The transformation I'm looking for may occur when all of Quebec society looks again at its past in a way that makes it possible to get away from a repertoire of stories.

In that regard, things are very interesting in Quebec at the present time. Passages to the future are being opened everywhere. I wouldn't be surprised if, ten years from now, the vision of the past that is being presented to students has begun to change. A new generation of think-ers·has entered the debate to reconsider and reformulate the question of Quebec-Canada – and many others.[16] It is my expectation that the consequences of such a generational turnover will be visible in the not-too-distant future.

Is a similar trend at work in the rest of Canada? I'm not in a position to answer that question, although I hope it is. I keep thinking that the country will have a future when it recognizes, rather than rejects, its historical specificity and updates its central metaphors accordingly. In that process of reimagining a country in a sort of balance between its past and its future, its possibilities and its utopias, historians and teach-ers can play a very important role, clearing intellectual spaces and providing guidance through them. What we need most in present times are people who are not trapped in obsolete narratives, mistaken identities, and univocal representations of the complexity of our country, not to say the world.

NOTES

This chapter is based on a paper titled 'Mémoire et récit de l'aventure historique du Québec chez les jeunes Québécois d'héritage canadien-français: Coup de sonde, amorce d'analyse des résultats, questionnements,' *Canadian Historical Review* 85, 2 (2004): 325–56.

1 See the Memory Project, www.dominion.ca.
2 SRC-Radio, *Trou de mémoire* [Radio documents], Société Radio-Canada, 1995.
3 This research has been conducted with Sabrina Moisan. Data upon which this paper is based are to be found at length in Moisan, 'Mémoire historique de l'aventure québécoise chez les jeunes franco-québécois d'héritage canadien-français: coup de sonde et analyse des résultats' (MA thesis, Université Laval, 2002). Although discussed with her, the argument presented here is mine.
4 Since writing this piece, working with colleagues from across the country I have received a generous grant to undertake research on Canadians and their pasts. See http://atlanticportal.hil.unb.ca/en/communities/canadian_pasts/index.php
5 I have recently begun this research on students of non-French backgrounds.
6 A new and controversial program, 'History and Citizenship Education,' will be implemented in September 2007. We will have to see if it will bring a new representation of the past – and, consequently, historical consciousness – to students' minds.
7 J. Létourneau, 'Nous-Autres les Québécois: La voix des manuels d'histoire,' *International Textbook Research* 18, 3 (1996): 269–87.
8 Gouvernement du Québec, Ministère de l'Éducation, Direction générale du développement pédagogique, *Programme d'études: Histoire du Québec et du Canada, 4ᵉ secondaire, formation générale et professionnelle* (Quebec, April 1982), 18.
9 *Se souvenir et devenir: Rapport du Groupe de travail sur l'enseignement de l'histoire* (Quebec: Ministry of Education, 1996) For a discussion of the

teaching of history in Quebec ten years after the release of the Lacoursière Report, see 'La rapport Lacoursière sur l'enseignement de l'histoire, dix ans après,' special issue of *Bulletin d'histoire politique* 14, 3 (2006).

10 It seems the situation is replicated in English Canada. See, for example, current research done by Ruth Sandwell.

11 Daniel Francis, *National Dreams: Myth, Memory and Canadian History* (Vancouver: Arsenal Pulp Press, 1997).

12 Jocelyn Létourneau, 'Trapped by Mistaken Identity,' *Globe and Mail*, 5 March 2001, A9.

13 See Gérard Bouchard, *La Nation au futur et au passé* (Montreal: VLB, 1999).

14 Jocelyn Létourneau, *A History for the Future: Rewriting Memory and Identity in Quebec* (Montreal and Kingston: McGill-Queen's University Press, 2004).

15 For a lengthly discussion on this, see my 'Pour une nouvelle métaphore de l'expérience historique canadienne,' *Canadian Issues*, October 2001, 8–11.

16 See Stéphane Kelly, ed., *Les idées mènent le Québec: Essais sur une sensibilité historique* (Quebec: Presses de l'Université Laval, 2002).

6 The Blossoming of Canadian Historical Research: Implications for Educational Policy and Content

CHAD GAFFIELD

Since the 1960s, historical research on Canada has moved from a marginal activity of a small number of scholars in a few universities to a central feature of all history departments across the country. The growth in activity has reflected not only the expansion of postsecondary education but also the increasing attention paid to Canada both in the undergraduate and graduate curriculum. Along with their counterparts in other disciplines, most history professors in Canada before the 1970s had received graduate education in Europe or the United States, and they offered their students a Eurocentric selection of courses that reflected their own research projects on Great Britain, France, Germany, and, to a lesser extent, the United States and other countries.

There were, of course, important exceptions to this pattern, as described by Carl Berger in his award-winning book *The Writing of Canadian History: Aspects of English-Canadian Historical Writing, 1900–1970*.[1] However, the fact that Berger could devote a complete chapter to each key figure attests to the small number of those who actually engaged in research on Canada's history during these decades. In contrast, descriptions of the writing of Canadian history in recent decades uniformly emphasize the proliferation of interests across multiple fields of research as an increasing number of historians educated in Canada made the study of Canada's past a key feature of the postsecondary landscape.

The rapidly increasing number of courses, theses, and professors focused on Canadian history, especially during the 1970s and 1980s, reflected the new sentiments, attitudes, and policies associated with the changing cultural, economic, and political environment of these decades. The lingering colonial mentality that had worked against taking

Canadian history seriously gave way to a determination 'to know ourselves' (as T. Symons insisted) in undergraduate and graduate programs supported by new funding opportunities.[2] The contrast between the 1960s and the early twentieth-first century is stark in terms of what is available to those interested in Canada's past. One early example of the changing world of historical research was the unprecedented research and publishing initiatives that began producing the *Dictionary of Canadian Biography* and the three-volume *Historical Atlas of Canada*. The key feature of such efforts was research-intensiveness. In contrast to previous projects that characteristically involved single scholars offering sweeping interpretations based on individual archival work, the rewriting of Canadian history during the closing decades of the twentieth century was also based on collaborative initiatives that sought to come to grips with as much evidence as possible about as many topics as possible. The result not only transformed university departments but also prepared the way, by the end of the twentieth century, for new museum exhibitions, television series, best-selling books, frequently visited web sites, and other opportunities for the general public to think about the making of Canada.

But how can we reconcile the impressive blossoming of Canadian historical research after the 1960s with the claim that Canadian history was 'killed' during these years or with journalistic reports about 'the end of history' by the year 2000? If the extent and intensity of research on Canada's past have increased so significantly in recent decades, why have we not all begun to celebrate the fact that we are truly beginning to know ourselves? One factor that helps explain this apparent contradiction is that, just as university departments began to take Canadian history seriously, school systems began to replace history courses with more contemporarily oriented social studies classes. In other words, the trajectory of growth at the postsecondary level was contrasted with one of decline in the schools; while historians and students in universities were increasingly focused on Canada's past, their counterparts in schools were paying less and less attention to historical topics.

While both trajectories resulted from quite distinct and complex forces, they included a similar critique of their respective curricula that had been taught in the postwar decades. Just as professors sought to revise a Eurocentric approach that treated Canada as a marginal colony not worth much attention on its own terms, teachers, school boards, and parents became less and less comfortable with textbooks that were out of sync with the rapidly changing character of Canadian society. During the 1960s and 1970s, the teaching of Canadian history as a narrative of elite, white leaders forging progress under British influence became less attractive in the context of an official embracing of diversity characterized by substantially revised immigration policies.[3] As classrooms increasingly reflected the changing times, especially in the major urban centres, schools turned away from the available history texts towards curriculum material that addressed concerns more immediate to the lives of their students. Rather than continue using history books with a British focus and ethnic stereotyping that did not prepare students for the profound changes of the 1960s, schools often introduced courses focused on contemporary issues in Canadian society.[4] One result was that compulsory Canadian history courses were replaced in schools just when they were being expanded in universities. In both cases, the changes were occurring in light of a rejection of the established presentation of Canadian history, and thus can be explained as distinct articulations of the same phenomenon rather than as contradictory and unrelated patterns.

The question that arises, of course, is why a new Canadian history curriculum quickly began taking shape in universities but not in the schools. One answer is that textbook writing virtually stopped at all educational levels. After a flurry of books published in the 1950s and 1960s, only a small number of Canadian history surveys for university courses appeared in the 1970s and 1980s, and none achieved widespread acceptance. Indeed, professors often moved away from textbooks during these years and characteristically taught courses using journal articles for required reading. While some professors combined one of the established survey texts with a selection of more recently published articles, they often used the text as a way to show the weaknesses of the older literature as much as to provide an overview for the course. In contrast, the structure of schools meant that teachers were more dependent on textbooks for the content of their classes. In the absence of instructional materials appropriate to their objectives, the understandable option was to eliminate the course.

The fact that textbook writing on Canadian history became so unattractive during the 1970s and 1980s reflected one of the most unanticipated results of the new and increasing interest in historical research: the impossibility of presenting syntheses of Canadian history in keeping with the established style of linear, chronologically ordered narration. Historians did not produce new surveys of Canadian history in these years simply because they did not see a way to do so in keeping with their research findings. This difficulty was not anticipated: historians thrust themselves into fields associated with what came to be called the 'new social history' on the assumption that their objective was to add the study of women, the poor, ethnic minorities, and other previously 'anonymous' groups to the established record of elite men acting as political, religious, and economic leaders. It became clear quickly, however, that the jigsaw-puzzle metaphor of increased understanding with the addition of each new historical 'piece' could not be sustained. In fact, each new study raised new questions about previous studies. Studies in the history of women undermined established conclusions about the history of men, just as research on the working class called into question the dominant interpretations of bourgeois history.

Rather than systematically producing an increasingly complete picture of the past, the new studies of the 1970s and 1980s pointed to the need to reconsider the entire framework of the established syntheses of Canadian history. One example of this development was the quite sudden disappearance of the notion of a 'definitive' study. Long-considered by authors as the highest praise for a study, this notion came to be rejected as inappropriate given the newly recognized distinction between 'history' and 'the past.' Historical studies were increasingly evaluated as much in terms of the questions they raised as the answers they suggested.[5] In this sense, research efforts were no longer viewed in terms of systematic progress towards comprehensive understanding, and thus the writing of overall interpretations became especially challenging.

In addition, the burst of Canadian historical research in the 1970s and 1980s worked against the writing of textbooks because scholars began developing new views of the character of historical change that did not fit comfortably within the familiar framework of key dates, events, and figures.[6] During these decades, historians gained appreciation of both the complexity and diversity of social, economic, cultural, and political change in different times and places. In the early years of the 'new social history,' scholars expected to be able to specify patterns for processes such as urbanization and industrialization by systematically studying places such as Montreal, Toronto, and Hamilton. This expectation proved difficult to fulfil, as each study revealed quite distinct contours of change.

Similar unexpected results across diverse historical topics undermined two key assumptions with which scholars had launched major research projects: that the examination of more evidence would clarify historical phenomena, and that the closer historians examined a topic, the clearer it would appear. These assumptions had underpinned the popularity of micro-history, in which scholars examined in detail specific historical contexts in light of specific historical evidence. This approach has proven to be an effective way of exploring how individuals, groups, and communities changed, and were changed by, social, economic, cultural, and political forces. But micro-historical studies revealed that understandings of such changes in different settings could not be easily added together to form macro-historical explanations. Each new study did not necessarily clarify the topic under investigation; in fact, new studies usually added new complexity to previous understandings and made historical phenomena more difficult to explain.[7]

Not only did scholars come to emphasize the interrelated character of historical phenomena, but they also found that these relationships were contingent in significant respects. One result was that historians began to use the plural more often than the singular when describing their topics. The study of 'literacy' was replaced by the study of 'literacies,' while projects on 'the family' gave way to research on 'families.' Similarly, historians began describing the 'multiple paths' of industrialization as well as further complicating the earlier description of 'limited identities' across Canada. The result was that nothing seemed truly representative of a larger phenomenon. No city adequately illustrated the process of urbanization, no workplace reflected the complete character of industrialization, and no township served as an adequate example of rural change. In this context, it became increasingly difficult to synthesize Canadian history; how could justice be done to the emerging view of historical change as multiple, uneven, contested, ambiguous, non-linear, and profoundly complex?[8]

Some observers misunderstood the extent to which scholars were developing fundamentally different concepts of Canadian history during the 1970s and 1980s, and they began blaming groups of historians for a perceived fragmentation of knowledge that was then linked to the small place occupied by history in the school curriculum. In this view, the new attention to women, minority groups, the poor, and others was not enriching historical understanding but was instead destroying its foundation. Such critics realized that the results of the new social history and similar work not only undermined the established assumptions about who made Canada but also called into question the appropriateness of overarching interpretations that did not take into account the deep diversity of individual and collective experience across the provinces and territories. The fact that historians were struggling to come to grips with such diversity made appealing to some the claim that researchers should return to earlier approaches, as their new work was fragmenting historical understanding rather than producing new syntheses. In fact, the serious challenge facing historians was to reinterpret Canada's past in light of the newly recognized complexity of historical change. During the 1970s, historians quickly dismantled the familiar framework of the established textbooks as both simplistic as well as sexist, racist, and socially biased.[9] It would be almost two decades before scholars felt ready to begin building new frameworks that could do justice to the significance of gender, class, ethnicity, and regional characteristics across Canada.

In my own case, I began seeing how the undergraduate history curriculum could be revised in keeping with the new historical research as a result of what educators call a 'teachable moment.' This expression refers to those special times when, usually unexpectedly, a great occasion for real learning occurs during a seminar or lecture or classroom discussion. The assumption of the expression 'teachable moment' is that students really learn something during those moments, often in unanticipated ways. However, the teachable moments I most remember are when I, as a professor, really learned something from my students; in this case, more than two hundred of them had come to a large lecture hall to hear me, as a sabbatical replacement, lecture on a topic about which I knew only the bare minimum. In addition to staying up until the wee hours the night before preparing the lecture, I was also trying to finish a conference paper that was to be presented at the annual meeting of the Learned Societies just weeks after the course ended. In preparing this paper, I was struggling to analyse the underlying individual-level patterns that might have given rise to some aggregate-level trends that I had identified using published census figures for the late nineteenth century. Perhaps out of a sense of desperation, I went to the lecture hall ahead of time and drew a table of figures on the blackboard that I then invited the arriving students to examine with me. In doing so, I was certainly feeling guilty. One of the few things I had ever been taught about teaching was that a clear distinction had to be made between your own research projects and your courses; in fact, a course that had a close relationship to a professor's research activities was disparaged as a 'vanity course.' One result was that, as an undergraduate, I had no idea what my professors were researching in the hours when they were not teaching. Professors certainly never told students in class what they were writing about, and while rumours might circulate that someone had published something, such talk never arose in the classroom.

But somehow that day in my lecture class felt better than any other. The students became animated as they tried to solve my research puzzle. And when I insisted that we finally begin the lecture, they seemed disappointed and I could sense them slip into passivity. Two months later, my guilt about taking time in class for my own research questions instead of lecturing for the full fifty minutes was completely alleviated when I read the course evaluations. For the students, the most memorable and important class had been that day. The student evaluations revealed how the students longed to look at historical evidence themselves, and, with my collaboration, to discover patterns, hypothesize about thought and behaviour, and then construct interpretations that had meaning for them. In light of such classroom experiences, I began to offer students more and more opportunities to engage in genuine historical research through primary sources as a way to allow them to construct knowledge actively rather than to absorb knowledge passively.

A second 'teachable moment' the following year further convinced me that the role of the professor was to help students on their journey of historical discovery and their construction of interpretations in keeping with the evidence. The setting was a large lecture class on twentieth-century Canada, and my lecture that day dealt with the Depression of the 1930s. In keeping with the historiographical spirit of the times, I tried not only to provide a survey of the major economic trends and policies but also to provide examples of the everyday life experiences of labouring men and women, as well as minority ethnic groups struggling in both rural and urban areas, and the limits of government action in the face of poverty and homelessness in certain parts of Canada. As usual, I had allocated fifteen minutes for questions, comments, and discussion after the lecture, and so when I summarized what I thought were the key points of my presentation, I invited the class to take advantage of this time, especially in light of an upcoming test. Immediately, a hand shot up in the back of the lecture hall. I was quite pleased when I realized that it belonged to a senior citizen who had registered as part of a new effort to attract retired individuals to the campus but who thus far had been silent and had appeared somewhat isolated from the much younger students in the class. So, I quickly called upon him, and he rose from his seat to proclaim loudly, 'That's not the way it was!'

In the following instant, I was reminded how, physiologically, the human body can go from a feeling of considerable satisfaction to one of absolute terror in a millisecond. The whole class turned to look at this senior citizen, and then turned back to look at me, and then turned back to look at him, and then to me. What should I say? It was instantly clear to everyone that this student had lived through the Depression and had first-hand knowledge of everyday life at that time in a way that I certainly did not. Would students no longer have confidence in my lectures? Was my career as a professor coming to a premature end? Happily, it was at this moment that I fully recognized that students should always be given the chance to see themselves or those like them in historical pictures of the past. I responded, 'Gee, that's interesting. Share with us your experience ...' And indeed he had a lot to tell. Over the next five minutes, he recounted how he always had a job during the 1930s by using his gumption and ingenuity, and, as a result of his willingness to work really hard, he was able to make ends meet. In his view, the 1930s might have been a challenge, but there was no need for governments to begin thinking that they had to control the economy or to guarantee the quality of life. His comments provoked quite a reaction among the other students as they probed more deeply into the context of his memories of the 1930s, and the discussion continued into the next class and indeed the rest of the course.

What I learned in this 'teachable moment' was that, in order to come to grips with historical change, you must be able to see yourself in the picture of the past.[10] Understandings of the various times and places must have meaning in your own life. In order to learn history, individuals must be able to relate to this 'foreign country' called the past.[11] After that day, I wondered how many other people in the class did not see themselves in my lecture of the 1930s, even though I had done my best to emphasize the diversity and complexity of the period. In the end, I knew that my lecture had not adequately emphasized the myriad ways in which different people in different places came to grips with the challenges of the decade. More importantly, perhaps, I had not communicated that 'history' is not definitive, and that everyone is invited to contribute to better historical understandings.

As an increasing number of historians like me were coming to grips with the fundamental pedagogical issues that arose from the new studies of Canadian history, the discipline began contributing to a transformation of undergraduate education. In stylized terms, this transformation can be described as the move from a transmission-of-knowledge model based on passive learning to a discovery-and-construction-of-knowledge model based on active learning. In the former model, students in history were expected to learn about the past by reading, memorizing, and recounting the portrayals and interpretations formulated by professional historians. While students did examine specific historical documents in this approach, genuine historical research was not a key feature of the curriculum.[12] Rather, students studied the past by reading the writings of historians, and by memorizing their content. This transmission-of-knowledge approach meant that primary sources did not play a major role in the educational system of the mid-twentieth century; the one exception was at the graduate level, when original research became the focus of attention.

By the later 1980s, however, an active-learning model was increasingly implemented in undergraduate education, and in this context historians began developing the new syntheses of Canadian history that became familiar during the 1990s.[13] Unlike earlier textbooks, the objective of these syntheses was to help students learn how to connect the new appreciations of historical diversity and complexity with macro-level understandings of Canadian history. In these volumes, historians suggested a new sense of historical specificity. Rather than seeing certain individuals or places or events as determining the distinctiveness of Canadian history, researchers increasingly suggested that the specificity of Canada was the result of unique convergences of non-unique phenomena across time and space. In other words, Canada was not defined by the presence of distinctive traits but rather by how characteristics familiar in other times and places came together in specific ways that, taken together, made Canada recognizable. In other words, macro-interpretations could be based on micro-historical diversity and complexity with the understanding that further research would continue to enrich and revise such overall explanations.

One key pedagogical strategy that became increasingly popular was to engage students in both primary and secondary sources. In this approach, students are expected not only to learn about the research results of historians but also to engage relevant primary sources in order to construct interpretations of the past that connect to their own lives. Rather than simply memorizing the conclusions of others, students are expected to engage historical evidence on their own terms with a view towards developing historical understandings that have meaning in their personal lives, thereby explicitly connecting micro and macro levels of understanding. The conceptual underpinnings of this approach have been considerably strengthened by research in learning theory that increasingly emphasizes the importance of active student participation in education. In fact, the findings of cognitive psychologists challenge the conventional belief that original scholarship best follows the mastery of current wisdom. Rather, researchers have now suggested that an exclusive focus on absorbing knowledge from 'experts' undermines, rather than enhances, the potential for subsequent creativity and innovation. The explanation for this phenomenon is that, when a teacher insists that students learn all the reasons for the location of the current research frontier, they are implicitly and effectively encouraged to think so much like their predecessors that they become less able to push the frontier to a new place. According to such cognitive theories, a secondary source–based undergraduate history curriculum undermines the potential (rather than lays the foundation) for original scholarship at the graduate level.

Although much more study needs to be done to understand the daunting processes of learning and creativity, the older transmission-of-knowledge structure of the history curriculum may help explain a series of consistent findings about higher education during the twentieth century, including, for example, the poor correlation between grades in courses and the subsequent research productivity of those who go on to become historians; the pattern of theoretical and methodological innovation coming from outside more than inside the history discipline; and the association of 'schools of thought' with history departments in specific universities. In this context, the increasing role of primary sources in undergraduate history courses reflects a profound change, as a result of which educators have begun rethinking the established distinctions between the baccalaureate, master's, and doctoral levels. Over the past decade, the emerging pattern is for all levels to adopt a discovery-and-construction-of-knowledge approach to the curriculum. In BA history programs, this approach combines, in a dialectical way, a back-and-forth, active and passive, engagement with both original research projects and current scholarly findings. In this sense, the baccalaureate is beginning to become a research degree.[14] Obviously, the objective of this degree is linked to graduate education for only a small minority of students. For the majority, the aim of a BA as a research degree continues to be the opportunity to develop an informed cultural and scientific framework and competency in order to lead a full and productive life as an engaged citizen interested in making a better world. In both cases, however, an increasing number of scholars are convinced that the active learning of history is the most effective way to construct lasting and meaningful historical knowledge.

At the same time, it would be misleading to imply that a strong consensus has already been reached among educators about the appropriate objectives and content of and methods for the history curriculum.[15] At the university level, debate continues about the relative merits of teaching and research, and some professors still believe that they are distinct activities involving quite different concepts and skills. The increased research intensiveness of universities is sometimes associated with an increasing neglect of teaching as a priority, especially at the undergraduate level. A common assumption is that professors see their own research as unrelated to their teaching and that, given the choice, they would simply focus on their own projects. In fact, however, the blossoming of Canadian historical research has been accompanied by a blossoming of interest in improving historical education for students; hence, the spread of course evaluations in the 1970s, centres for university teaching in the 1980s, and formal courses on university teaching in the 1990s. As research activities intensified, so did efforts to enhance the educational experience of students.

The connection between historical teaching and research is worth emphasizing, as it is often assumed that professors teach only to the extent required officially whereas they undertake research on their own initiative. Some perspective on this issue is provided by the example of the Committee on Preparing a Program for Research and Publication, a group formed in 1927 by the American Historical Association. This committee sent questionnaires to five hundred holders of PhD degrees in history who were teaching at the postsecondary level in the United States. The first two questions were: 'What in your opinion is the obligation or duty of a doctor of philosophy in history to teaching on the one hand and research on the other?' and 'What is the attitude of the president of the institution where you now hold a position toward research as compared to teaching?' The results showed that 'The opinion is almost unanimous that the main duty of a Ph.D. is to teach' and that 'at least 50% of the Presidents are hostile, or so lukewarm that little real encouragement is given to professors who wish to carry on with research. Either they are told that research is not expected or wanted; or if a professor does produce, no notice is taken of his work ... as compared with the recognition given to teaching or to administrative work.' The committee reported that 'most Ph.D.s prefer the human contacts with their students or with their colleagues to the isolation, steady grind, and slowness of reward which are inevitably the lot of the man who sticks to productive scholarship. In other words, the average doctor of philosophy does not want to be a greasy grind all his life. He has to be till he gets his doctor's degree, and in many cases, he says, "Thank God, I have got it" and he quits research activity to focus exclusively on teaching.'[16]

The example of the American Historical Association's concerns about research in the 1920s emphasizes the significance of developments in Canada during recent decades. Rather than competing with each other, teaching and research have both blossomed with the blossoming of Canadian history, because these two activities have increasingly become intimately interrelated in a new paradigm of historical scholarship. Teaching and research are becoming two articulations of the same process, the process of discovery and construction of knowledge. When professors guide students engaging in this process, we call it teaching; when professors engage in it themselves (and perhaps in collaboration with students), we call it research. This is why some historians reject the dichotomy of teaching and research in favour of the comprehensive concept of historical scholarship.

It was in this changed conceptual context that computerization began accelerating the transformation of the discipline of history. Unlike the 1960s, when controversy raged about the appropriateness of computer-based historical research, the subsequent decades have witnessed the computerization of almost all aspects of historical teaching and research.[17] The key point, however, is that the stage was set for the integration of computers into scholarly and educational activity by new conceptualizations of the past and of cognitive development. In this sense, computerization has been facilitating and enhancing a development that was already underway for substantive reasons.

The claim that the current educational change is not primarily a technological issue may be surprising, as so much debate has focused on developments such as the proliferation of mainframe computers in the 1970s, personal computers in the 1980s, and the Internet in the 1990s. However, none of these technologies would have proliferated to the same extent if they had not been propelled by forceful conceptual change. Just as the typewriter became pervasive only after reconceptualizations of the workplace, computerization in history has become increasingly important in light of the new attitudes towards learning and research.

The changing character of historical scholarship is also calling for new horizontal connections between history departments, archives, and other institutions including libraries and museums. The separate 'vertical' structures that were built during the nineteenth and twentieth centuries had the effect of developing a segmented research world composed of distinct parts with their own cultures, organizational values, and professional associations. For researchers, it was assumed that libraries held secondary sources organized by subject while archives held primary sources organized by provenance. In practice, this assumption never did justice to the actual workings of either institution, where overlaps in the nature of holdings became familiar and where efforts were made to organize material intellectually by both creator and subject. Nonetheless, changes in the late twentieth century began exposing the artificiality of not connecting the different priorities and organizational choices evident in the distinct institutional structures associated with historical teaching and research. It is in this sense that a new model of a horizontally connected continuum began inspiring the building of computer-based research infrastructures within which electronic archives are taking a central place along with digital libraries, virtual museums, and other electronic repositories of historical material. These new infrastructures enable the discovery and construction of knowledge not only by researchers able to visit repositories but also by students, who can remotely engage primary sources in unprecedented ways.[18] For this reason, lessons on the evaluation of web sites, on search-engine strategies, and on the analysis of databases are some of the new features of history courses at different educational levels. Moreover, surveys of how children develop their historical consciousness emphasize the importance of situating formal history classes within a much larger social context of learning about the past. For this reason, the extent to which computerization can enhance the horizontal connections across vertical institutional structures will help determine the impact of Canadian historical research on public memory.

It should be emphasized that the cultural and institutional obstacles on the path to building comprehensive virtual infrastructures for historical scholarship remain substantial and may even be increasing as we learn more about the complex questions raised by this new era. Included among these are issues of intellectual property, recognition, authenticity, preservation, and national and international cooperation on issues such as standards. And there is the question of financial support, as the new approaches clearly are more costly than those in the transmission-of-information model. In this sense, it is not surprising that many departments of history offer undergraduate and graduate curricula that look much as they did many years ago. Introductory lecture courses and upper-level seminars based on secondary sources remain the predominant features of undergraduate programs in many universities. In the context of inadequate resources, the potential for curriculum change in history has only begun to be realized in a minority of programs. Even worse, the deteriorating student-professor ratios in many departments of history have worked against research-oriented initiatives and have favoured the use of multiple-choice tests and rote learning as a way to accommodate inappropriately large classes. In this sense, the debate about history is part of the debate about universities, and by thinking about changes in the discipline of history, we are engaging the larger debate about the future of higher education. Similarly, the debate about history is part of the debate about schools and their role in society.[19] Clearly, a great deal of work remains to be done to ensure that the blossoming of Canadian historical scholarship continues to move forward debates about educational policy and content, and, most importantly, to enhance our individual and collective understandings of Canada's past.

NOTES

1 Carl Berger, *The Writing of Canadian History: Aspects of English-Canadian Historical Writing, 1900–1970* (Toronto: Oxford University Press, 1976).
2 T.H.B. Symons, *To Know Ourselves: The Report of the Commission of Canadian Studies* (Ottawa: Association of Universities and Colleges Canada, 1975–84).
3 Jose E. Igartua, 'A Million Copies: George Brown's Canadian History School Texts as *de facto* National History Textbooks, 1942–1966,' paper presented to the Annual Meeting of the Canadian Historical Association, Winnipeg, 3 June 2004.
4 For example, see Ken Montgomery, '"A Better Place to Live": Representations of Knowledge about Racism and Its Oppositions in Canadian History Textbooks,' paper presented to the Annual Meeting of the Canadian Historical Association, Winnipeg, 3 June 2004.
5 For example, the impact of Louise Dechêne's work is examined in Sylvie Dépatie, *Habitants et Marchands Twenty Years Later: Reading the History of Seventeenth- and Eighteenth-Century Canada* (Montreal: McGill-Queen's University Press, 1998).

6 Bernard Bailyn, 'The Challenge of Modern Historiography,' *American Historical Review* 87, no. 2 (1982): 1–24.

7 Chad Gaffield, 'Historical Thinking, C.P. Snow's Two Cultures, and a Hope for the 21st Century,' *Journal of the Canadian Historical Association* (Spring 2002): 3–25.

8 John Bonnett has revealed how Harold Innis anticipated key features of twentieth-century historiographical developments. Bonnett pursues Innis's insights in work such as 'Bringing Students to a Virtual Past: Teaching Ottawa History with the 3D Historical Cities Project,' in Jeff Keshen and Nicole St-Onge, eds., *Construire une capitale – Ottawa – Making a Capital* (Ottawa: University of Ottawa Press 2001), 483–502.

9 See Timothy J. Stanley, 'Why I Killed Canadian History: Towards an Anti-Racist History in Canada,' *Histoire sociale/Social History* 33, no. 65 (2001): 79–103, and chapter 3 in this volume.

10 For a stimulating discussion in the context of the National Archives of Canada, see Ian E. Wilson, 'First Person, Singular ... First Person, Plural: Making Canada's Past Accessible,' *Canadian Issues* (October 2003).

11 David Lowenthal, *The Past Is a Foreign Country* (Cambridge: Cambridge University Press, 1985).

12 Ken Osborne's work has included fascinating discussions of efforts to use primary sources in the teaching of history during the late nineteenth and early twentieth centuries, as he indicates in chapter 7 in this volume as well.

13 Linda Kealey, Ruth Pierson, Joan Sangster, and Veronica Strong-Boag, 'Teaching Canadian History in the 1990s: Whose "National" History Are We Lamenting?' *Journal of Canadian Studies* 27, no. 2 (1992): 129–36.

14 Chad Gaffield, 'Primary Sources, Historical Thinking, and the Emerging Redefinition of the B.A. as a Research Degree,' *Facsimile* nos. 23–5 (2000–1): 12–17.

15 Margaret Conrad and Alvin Finkel, 'Textbook Wars: Canadian Style,' *Canadian Issues* (October 2003): 12–15.

16 Marcus W. Jernegan, 'Productivity of Doctors of Philosophy in History,' *American Historical Review* 33, no. 1 (1927): 1–22. Many thanks to Dr. Jo-Anne McCutcheon for bringing this article to my attention.

17 Chad Gaffield, 'Machines and Minds: Historians and the Emerging Collaboration,' *Histoire sociale/Social History* 21, no. 42 (1988): 312–17.

18 Wilson J. Warren, 'Using the World Wide Web for Primary Source Research in High School History Classes,' *Journal of the Association for History and Computing* 2, no. 2 (1999). Available at http://www.mcel.pacificu.edu/JAHC/JAHC112/warren/warren.html

19 Ken Osborne, 'Teaching History in Schools: A Canadian Debate,' *Journal of Curriculum Studies* 35, no. 5 (2003): 585–626.

7 'To the Past': Why We Need to Teach and Study History

KEN OSBORNE

In the mid-1980s, looking for something that would alert students to the importance of history, I reread George Orwell's *Nineteen Eighty-Four*. It had been at least twenty years since I had last read it, and what I found surprised me. The more I read, the more it dawned on me that the novel is a profound meditation on the power of history. We all know that one of the central characteristics of the regime described in *Nineteen Eighty-Four* is its incessant rewriting of history. Orwell was making a point when he made the novel's central character, Winston Smith, a worker at the Ministry of Truth, where his job was to rewrite history according to party directives. If he had simply wanted to make a point about totalitarian dictatorship, Orwell could have made Winston a member of the thought police or assigned him to another ministry, such as Peace or Love. Winston's lover, Julia, for example, also worked at the Ministry of Truth, but her job was to produce soft pornography for the proles, and Orwell never tells us any more about it, whereas he describes Winston's work in great detail. Orwell wanted to make a point about the power of history, and his point was that without an accurate knowledge and understanding of history, we are doomed to be victims of manipulation at best and subjugation at worst.

This is obviously the point of the official slogan of the party: 'Who controls the past controls the future: who controls the present controls the past.' On several occasions in the novel Orwell addresses this point directly, as, for example, when Winston tries to convince Julia of the importance of the past: 'Do you realize that the past, starting from yesterday, has actually been abolished? ... Every record has been destroyed or falsified, every book has been rewritten, every picture has been repainted, every statue and street and building has been renamed, every date had been altered. And that process is continuing day by day and minute by minute. History has stopped. Nothing exists except an endless present in which the party is always right. I know, of course, that the past is falsified, but it would never be possible for me to prove it, even when I did the falsification myself. The only evidence is in my own mind, and I don't know with any certainty that any other human being shares my memories.'[1]

In fact, the position was more desperate than Winston indicated. Not only did people not share his memories; they did not even think about the past. Winston himself wondered at one point, 'Was he, then, alone in the possession of a memory?' (50). Julia told him that the past was neither useful nor interesting. Perhaps as a result, she was not interested in the future either, living only for the day itself, a revolutionary from the waist down, in Winston's graphic phrase.

Winston was unable to live this way, even though his inability to close his mind to the past made him a misfit in his own society and a danger to its government. Time and again, fragmentary memories came to him: he dreamed of his mother and sister, of the Golden Country of his childhood, of the time before the revolution. Without conscious effort, he compared past and present. In the Ministry of Truth cafeteria, 'He meditated resentfully on the state of affairs. Had it always been like this? Had food always tasted like this?' (51). Orwell piles on depressing description after depressing description, ending with this thought in Winston's head: 'Why should one feel it to be intolerable unless one had some kind of ancestral memory that things had once been different?' (51). Winston's problem was that he had too many such memories: his interest in the past would not leave him and eventually it dragged him down. When he went to the apartment of the party boss, O'Brien, in the mistaken belief that O'Brien was really a secret dissident, Winston responded to his suggestion for a toast to humanity, or the death of Big Brother, or the confusion of the thought police, or even the future, with a suggestion of his own: 'To the past' (144). And the ultimate irony of the novel is Winston's final interrogation by O'Brien, with the accusation that Winston's fundamental problem was that he suffered from 'a defective memory' (197).

In these and countless other ways Orwell tells us that the past does matter, that we forget it at our peril, and that if we do forget or dismiss it we give up one of the most powerful tools we have to preserve a decent present and create a better future. Reading *Nineteen Eighty-Four* made me think of the many ways that history impinges on our thinking and provides us with associations, connections, and points of reference that simultaneously take us beyond our present context and give us a way of viewing it from the outside, as it were. It gives us at one and the same time a sense both of attachment and of detachment, while also helping us arm ourselves against those who seek to control us, whether mentally or physically.

Consider, for example, an everyday journey from my house in South Winnipeg to the centre of the city. We begin in St Norbert, a name and place that connects with the Metis and fur-trade traditions of Manitoba, for it began as a Metis community in the nineteenth century, and also with the long history of the Roman Catholic Church, for Norbert was also one of the names of Joseph-Norbert Provencher, who came to Red River as a missionary in 1818 and eventually became its bishop. From St Norbert we travel along Pembina Highway, two words with a host of historical associations. 'Pembina' takes us back to the long Aboriginal history of Manitoba, to the fur trade, and to the establishment of the forty-ninth parallel as the border between British North America and the United States in 1818. 'Highway' is a word that takes us back to the Middle Ages and in a sense back to the world of ancient Roman roads. Along this stretch of Pembina Highway we find a host of names with historical associations – the Victoria Hospital, the Montcalm Hotel, the Renaissance Apartments, the Round Table Restaurant, Vincent Massey School, a Lutheran church, the Louis Riel Apartments – and other institutions, including a police station, a post office, and a public library, that remind us of the nineteenth-century transformation of municipal government.

We also pass signs for the University of Manitoba, where two sets of associations come into play. The word 'university' takes us back to medieval Europe and the first universities, with many of the same titles and rituals: bachelors, masters, doctors, lectures, professors, faculties, rectors, provosts, chancellors, and the rest. At the same time, the word 'Manitoba' reminds us of thousands of years of Aboriginal history, while also connecting us with the creation of the province of Manitoba in 1870 and all its associations with the wider history of Canada. This part of Pembina Highway also runs through Fort Garry, once a free-standing municipality and now part of the city of Winnipeg, whose name reminds us once again of Manitoba's Aboriginal history and also of the creation of Winnipeg as a unified city in the 1960s. In addition, the name 'Fort Garry' takes us back to the fur trade and, more specifically, to the conflict between the Northwest Company and the Hudson's Bay Company, which ended with their amalgamation in 1821, when Nicholas Garry came to Red River to supervise the union of the two companies.

If we look across the Red River as we head downtown, we see the buildings of the St Boniface area, a name that is particularly rich in historical connections. The historical figure St Boniface began life as Wynfrith, one of those determined English missionaries who went to pagan Germany in the eighth century. Killed by those he was trying to convert, he earned a posthumous reputation as the patron saint of Germany. His name was brought to Red River by the largely Swiss-German De Meurons soldiers brought out by Lord Selkirk in 1816 to protect his settlement. Here is another train of associations, for the De Meurons were veterans of the Napoleonic Wars in Europe and had been sent to Canada to fight in the War of 1812. Discharged in Montreal at the end of that war, some of them were recruited by Lord Selkirk as his private army. Some of them stayed in Red River, which temporarily earned the name of Germantown, and it was their presence that prompted the Catholic priests who arrived in 1818 to bestow the name 'St Boniface,' with its German connections, on their new parish.

There is no need to belabour the point. I have described only a few of the historical connections that arise during this journey, which could be repeated almost anywhere in Canada. But rereading Orwell's *Nineteen Eighty-Four* some twenty years ago made me think about how important such connections are. At a trivial, but not to be despised, level, they make life more interesting. They add imagination and interest to what is otherwise humdrum routine. More important, they connect us with a world beyond our own and give us a point of reference that lies beyond the here-and-now concerns of the present. They provide us with a sense of perspective and proportion. In a sense they no doubt smack of antiquarianism, but there is more to be said for antiquarianism than its critics allow. Antiquarians are said to be fusty and dry-as-dust, uncritically obsessed with the trivialities of bygone ages, and thus very different from the critically aware practitioners of up-to-date historical method, though in my experience antiquarians generally prove to be enormously interesting people who can bring the past to life. The line commonly drawn between antiquarianism and history is overdrawn. At the heart of antiquarianism, after all, lies an interest in, even an obsession with, the past, not for what it tells us about the present or for its illumination of human affairs, but simply because it exists. At the heart of every historian one finds an antiquarian. If they were not interested in the past they study, historians could hardly do their work at all. And antiquarianism has the merit of taking us outside ourselves, of reminding us that we are the heirs of the past and, therefore, trustees for the future.

Even more important – and here is the relevance of Orwell – the kinds of everyday historical associations I have described buttress a sense of personal autonomy that is also rooted in the human experience. Such associations were what Winston Smith and everyone else needed if they were to withstand the manipulations of Big Brother. They provide a sense of membership in and continuity with the human story. In *Nineteen Eighty-Four,* Winston realized that he and others were 'lifted clean out of the stream of history' (134). And this is precisely the point. We are in the stream of history whether we like it or not, and if we are to negotiate its currents successfully we need the kind of navigation guide that a knowledge of history can provide. We need to situate ourselves knowledgeably in the stream of history to avoid being swept away. Perhaps the central point of Orwell's novel is its depiction of what can happen to a society where people have no knowledge of or connection with history. This is why the teaching of history matters.

In Canada one can distinguish three conceptions of what it means to teach and study history, all of which are still in play to varying degrees. One is the nation-building, narrative approach that dominated Canadian schools from the 1890s to the 1970s and is still very much alive, especially but not only in the elementary grades. The second appeared early in the twentieth century but in Canada began to make its presence felt in any significant way only in the 1970s. It approaches history not as a narrative of nation building but rather as the analysis of contemporary problems in their historical context. The third also has long roots but came to prominence in Canada only in the 1990s and sees history education as the process by which students come to understand history as a form of disciplined inquiry and thereby learn to think historically. In what follows I will call them HE 1, HE 2, and HE 3, respectively.

The central characteristic of HE 1 is its conception of history as the narrative of nation building. When I began teaching in Winnipeg in 1961, for example, the authorized textbook bore the title *Building the Canadian Nation.* First published in 1942, it was still in use in revised form in the 1960s. Its title describes its message, and indeed that of all other textbooks of its day, at least in English-speaking Canada. Canada either already was a nation or was well on the way to becoming one. In either case, its history was the story of its building: geographically by explorers, fur traders, and others; economically by merchants, railway builders, industrialists, and the like; demographically by successive waves of immigrants; and politically by statesmen and politicians. This narrative avoided the chest-beating we-are-the-greatest message found in some other countries, but its central theme was clear, even if understated: Canadians had much to be proud of, and they should respect past generations for making the present possible. To put it another way, good citizens needed to know their country's history.

This nation-building story of the Canadian past always had its critics, but by the 1970s it was running into serious trouble. Some commentators exposed its many gaps and omissions, coming close to describing it as racist, sexist, class-based, and tendentious. In the words of a survey of Ontario history texts, it was teaching not history, but 'prejudice.'[2] Others pointed to its failure to keep abreast of developments in the discipline of history, especially at a time when a new social history of women, workers, the First Nations, and ethnic and cultural minorities seemed to be sweeping all before it. The dominant nation-building narrative was in large part (though not to the extent that its critics sometimes claimed) a history-from-above of political and social elites. The new history was very much a history-from-below of so-called ordinary people. Indeed, in the 1990s, one new history textbook carried the not-so-inspiring title *Ordinary Canadians*. Pedagogically, the nation-building narrative of HE 1 stood accused of boring students and turning history into little more than the memorization of barely understood names, dates, and events. A whole series of reports and investigations, starting in 1923 and running through 1930, 1933, 1945, 1953, 1962, and 1968, bore witness to the fact that students neither liked nor understood Canadian history, nor were they gaining anything useful from studying it.[3]

According to an influential 1968 report on history teaching across Canada – depressingly entitled *What Culture? What Heritage?* – the main thing students were learning in their Canadian history classes was to dislike Canadian history and, by extension, Canada itself. As *What Culture? What Heritage?* put it, the vast majority of students were nothing more than 'desk-bound listeners.' In science they did experiments and explored hypotheses; in mathematics they solved problems; in language and literature they wrote original prose and poetry; in physical education they did exercises and played games; in history, they sat, listened, and memorized. This narrowly didactic pedagogy was not inherent in the nation-building narrative of HE 1, but by the 1960s it had acquired an examination-based inertia that made it difficult to change. Good teachers did not fall victim to it, but, according to *What Culture? What Heritage?*, good history teaching was to be found in only 7 per cent of Canada's classrooms. Whatever the accuracy of this statistic, it did serious damage to the status of HE 1.

However, the most damning criticism of HE 1 by the 1970s was that it had not apparently worked. It had conspicuously failed to bridge the gap between English-speaking Canada and francophone Quebec, where English-Canada's version of nation-building history was seen as an assimilative threat. After some seventy or eighty years of nation-building history designed to strengthen national unity, Canada seemed to be in danger of falling apart. What English-speaking Canadians celebrated as a hundred years of progress, Québécois nationalists dismissed as 'cents ans d'injustice.' According to such historically informed commentators as George Grant and Donald Creighton, writing in the 1960s, Canada's first hundred years could well be its last.[4]

Defenders of HE 1 might have argued (though none did) that in reality their approach to history had never been tried. Despite the nation building rhetoric of ministerial pronouncements and curricula, teachers and students alike treated history as something to be covered rather than celebrated. In the real world of the classroom, as I discovered as a high school teacher in the 1960s, the primary goal was to pass the provincial examination. Students' futures and teachers' professional reputations depended on it. And provincial examinations said nothing about nation building. To quote the historian Hilda Neatby, writing in 1944, they were 'mere tests of mechanical memorization.' They both shaped and reflected curricula that, in the words of a 1953 survey, were 'factualized to the point of boredom.' As the historian W.L. Morton observed in 1953, there was a conspicuous difference between the introductions and preambles to curriculum documents and their content. The former spoke of citizenship and other noble goals; the latter consisted of lists of facts. Morton found the explanation for this dichotomy in the fact that the introductions were written by educationists and Ministry of Education staff, while the actual curricula were drawn up by committees of specialist teachers and university advisers. If there is such a thing as teaching history for its own sake (and as Keith Barton says in this volume, it is difficult to see what the sake of history is), provincial examinations embodied it. Their questions were remorselessly factual. They asked about the seigneurial system or the 1837 rebellions or the origins of Confederation and other such topics but never required students to put them in any kind of context or to work with historical data and evidence.[5]

But even if schools had taught nation-building history, it is more than likely that their success would have been limited at best. Any country that depends on its schools for the establishment of national identity and national unity is likely to be disappointed. Schools are simply not that influential. One does not have to be a Marxist to realize that schools largely follow society, they rarely lead it. The Soviet Union taught the principles of Soviet-style Marxism-Leninism and Marxist-Leninist history in its schools from the late 1920s to the late 1980s, and did so with all the resources of a coercive state and party at its command. But when the Soviet Union collapsed in 1991, its citizens simply turned their backs on the history they had studied in school. In a much more open society such as Canada, where students spend more time in front of the television than they do reading history books, it is unlikely that we will be much more successful. It is a matter of common experience that we forget most of what we study in school, especially when we have no occasion to use it in life. I recently came across a small volume of student reminiscences from the Winnipeg high school where I taught through the 1960s and early 1970s. I found myself mentioned twice. The first gratifyingly described my ability to bring the past to life. The second mentioned an occasion that I do not remember at all when apparently I made my reputation by lifting a broken desk above my head with one hand and hoisting it out of the room. It confirmed something that I realized when my own children attended school: what strikes students about their teachers is often not what teachers expect or even intend. As researchers have made clear, there can be a world of difference between the curriculum-as-written and the curriculum-as-taught, which in turn can be very different from the curriculum-as-experienced-by-students.

In any event, by the 1970s HE 1 was in trouble. Its perceived weaknesses and imperfections combined with developments in educational theory to open the way for a new approach to history education that I will call HE 2. It came in two forms, both originating in the United States. One was driven in large part by post-Sputnik panic and was intended to boost the intellectual rigour of American schools in order to meet alleged Soviet superiority in science and related subjects by organizing curricula around the 'structure of the disciplines' as defined by leading scholars. The other was a response to the student activism and social movements of the 1960s and aimed to strengthen democracy by teaching students how to analyse and respond to contemporary problems. The first approach saw history education largely as a matter of teaching students the 'mode of inquiry' employed by historians and replaced textbooks with collections of documents that required students to work out for themselves what happened in the past. The second saw history education as a matter of analysing contemporary problems ('public issues' was the phrase of choice) and persisting themes by using concepts and methods of investigation drawn from the social sciences, of which history was seen as one component. Despite initial interest and a fair amount of rhetorical support, the structure-of-the-disciplines approach made only a small impact on Canadian classrooms, though it did to some extent popularize the use of primary sources in teaching history. By contrast, the public-issues approach proved much more popular with teachers and became the foundation of the HE 2 approach to teaching history.[6]

Whereas HE 1 saw its contribution to citizenship as the inculcation of a sense of heritage and a general knowledge of the past, HE 2 took a more activist view and spoke in terms of giving the young the tools to analyse the problems facing their society in the present and in the conceivable future. In doing so, it made the past the servant of the present, treating it as a source of case studies and examples for the illumination of current problems. It focused on the analysis of political and social problems and the development of 'political literacy.' It emphasized not factual knowledge but the attainment of skills and the understanding of concepts. In the language used by educationists at the time, it favoured 'process' over 'product,' though it is difficult to see just how the two can ever be separated. In part, it was an understandable reaction to the sterile pedagogy associated with HE 1; in part, a response to what critics saw as the weaknesses of representative democracy. Its model citizen was the informed participant in the political process.

This approach was not entirely new. In the 1920s, as American schools began to absorb history into an interdisciplinary social studies, they replaced some history courses with courses in what were called 'community civics' and 'problems of democracy' that were often organized around 'real-life' problems. Before the 1920s, for example, the model high school history program in the United States was a four-year sequence of ancient history, medieval and modern Europe, British history, and American history, starting in Grade 9 and ending in Grade 12. By the 1930s the preferred model had become a year of community civics, then European (including ancient and British) history, followed by

American history, and ending with problems of democracy. Canadian schools in the 1970s did not adopt this pattern, but they broadly followed its lead by either absorbing history into a social studies approach, often in the form of the new subject of 'Canadian studies,' loosely based on sociology, or organizing it around social science concepts and themes such as power and authority, decision making, identity, human rights, and the like. As a result, history became less a chronological survey of the past and more the examination and analysis of problems, themes, and concepts, in which chronology was largely ignored. The standard topics of Canadian history were still taught, but they were approached differently. Not least, HE 2 lent itself to a pedagogy that educationists described by such words as inquiry, discovery, or dialogue. If nothing else, it offered students space to think and reflect, and in some versions to act, which traditional approaches to HE 1 largely denied them. Ideally, the student-as-researcher replaced the student-as-reciter and the teacher-as-mentor replaced the teacher-as-lecturer. It is perhaps worth noting that all the classes (all 7 per cent of them) described as doing good work in the 1968 survey, *What Culture? What Heritage?*, were using this approach.

The jury is still out on the question of whether HE 2 is more effective than HE 1, though cynics might well argue that it could hardly be less, but it proved popular with innovative teachers, especially once provincial examinations were eliminated in the 1970s. Even so, HE 2 never totally replaced HE 1, and many schools found ways to adopt what they saw as the best of both approaches. For example, they rethought chronological narrative so that it spoke more directly to contemporary problems, linked it more closely to students' experience, and taught it through a more student-centred pedagogy, using techniques such as simulation and role play, assignments requiring genuinely original research, the analysis of sources of evidence, and the like.

In recent years, a third approach has begun to make its presence felt.[7] Beginning in the United Kingdom in the 1960s, HE 3 has some obvious similarities with the structure-of-the-disciplines approach pioneered in those years in the United States. In some ways it represents an unknowing return to a conception of history education first advanced in the 1890s. Between the 1890s and the 1910s historians were united in insisting that there should be some use of primary sources in school history classes, though they did not agree on just what this entailed. For the majority it meant using primary sources as supplementary to a textbook in order to add interesting detail to the necessarily bare-bones summary of the text while also giving students a simple introduction to the raw materials of history. There was, however, a more pedagogically radical minority, such as Mary Sheldon Barnes of Stanford, Fred Morrow Fling of the University of Nebraska (whose sourcebooks were known in Canada), and, to a lesser extent, Oxford's Maurice Keatinge (whose 1910 text on teaching history was used in a number of Canadian normal schools), who wanted to see sources not supplementing but replacing textbooks.[8] In their view the study of history was not the memorization of facts but the study of evidence. They saw history not as the recital of the facts of the past but as the study of problems, whether substantive (what happened?) or evidentiary (what can we know for sure?).

Moreover, historians such as Barnes, Fling, and Keatinge were convinced, through their work in schools, that even relatively young students could do this kind of work with appropriate teaching. In their view, it would bring the study of history into line with what historians actually did and make it more interesting for students to learn and teachers to teach, while, not least, opening up a new discipline of history education to which teachers would be the main contributors, thereby turning teaching into a truly research-driven profession. In the event, however, this approach to the teaching of history proved to be too radical for the schools. For one thing, it demanded a higher level of education and training and greater access to resources than most teachers possessed. For another, it flew in the face of the expository, nation-building approach to history that policy makers in education endorsed. And, at a more mundane level, it was incompatible with the examination system that before the 1970s prevailed in all provinces and territories, where the imperatives of uniform marking on a province-wide basis meant that questions were confined to whatever could be marked 'objectively' (and cheaply), which meant that they called for the recital of factual information and nothing more.

HE 3 differs from HE 1 and HE 2 in seeing history primarily as a form of intellectual training rather than as an education for citizenship. Above all, it sees the purpose of history education as the initiation of students into history as a form of disciplined inquiry. Its primary concern is the development of historical thinking or, in Peter Seixas's phrase, historical consciousness. It sees this as history's distinctive contribution to the education of citizens. In its purest form, HE 3 treats citizenship as a useful but incidental benefit of studying history, but less purist approaches are prepared to give citizenship a more central role. Either way, proponents of HE 3 agree that the most compelling reason for teaching history in schools is to teach students to think historically. They see the study of history as important not because it in some way shapes society but because it shapes students. Initially, the pedagogical result was an emphasis not on the accumulation of facts, or the analysis of contemporary problems, but on the nature and use of evidence. Yet, over the years this equating of historical thinking with historical method has been broadened to approach something like a more sophisticated version of the historical mindedness that was first propounded in the 1890s, as demonstrated by Peter Seixas's description of historical consciousness in chapter 1 of this volume.

The justification for HE 3 is to be found in three sources: educational theory, psychology, and historiography. So far as educational theory is concerned, HE 3 is part of a tradition that dates back to the seven liberal arts of the ancient and medieval world and that sees education as a process of initiation into disciplined ways of thinking. In this view, the disciplines (or groups of related disciplines such as the social sciences or the natural sciences) are not accidental creations but the embodiment of distinctive and valuable ways of making sense of the world, with unique conceptual frameworks, methods of inquiry, and standards of proof. Further, to be truly educated means understanding, at least in a basic way, how each of the disciplines works. Thus, to learn history is not to learn the results of historians' research as distilled through monographs or textbooks but rather to understand how they go about their work – how they make sense of their data and use it to advance an interpretation or explore a hypothesis. To put it another way, to study history is to learn what questions to ask, not to parrot someone else's answers.

Psychologically, the HE 3 perspective means taking students seriously. The nation-building narrative of HE 1 by and large treated students as blank slates on which textbook writers, curriculum designers, teachers, and others could write whatever they chose. More or less explicitly, it equated learning with absorbing what an authority, be it teacher or textbook, had to impart. HE 2, for its part, took seriously the claims of Piagetian researchers in the 1970s that most students were too intellectually immature to understand history. To use Piagetian language, history demanded formal operational thought, but most students were concrete operational, or even pre-operational, thinkers. In the more accessible language of the British psychologist E.A. Peel, history demanded explainer or possibility-invoking thinking, but most students were only context-bound describers.[9] This was one reason why HE 2 turned to the study of contemporary problems and why, decades earlier, American educationists had abandoned history for community civics and problems of democracy. The theory was that students would see more 'relevance' in the problems of the here and now than in the past, while also finding them easier to understand. The logic of the 'expanding horizons' approach has dominated social studies and displaced history in the early grades since the 1930s. In this approach, young children start with the concrete reality of the family, the school, and the local community, and gradually move out into the wider world. As Simon Fraser's Kieran Egan has persuasively and repeatedly argued, this approach totally ignores the reality that even young children can deal with the unknown and the abstract in their own way: hence the popularity of dinosaurs, monsters, fairy tales, and for that matter Thomas the Tank Engine and his talking locomotive friends.[10] Nonetheless, we seem to be fixated on the idea that children can learn only by beginning with what is familiar and tangible. Following the old (but not necessarily true) maxim that in teaching we should move from the known to the unknown, proponents of HE 2 believed that students could best understand the past by moving backwards in time from the present. It is an idea that has a long lineage in history education. There were those in the 1890s, for example, who argued that the best way to teach history was to begin with the known present and, through a process of reverse chronology, move backwards in time. Indeed, some historians write history this way.

HE 3 sees students differently. It sees them not as blank slates but as active makers of meaning with their own ideas about history and the past. British researchers, for example, are identifying a developmental sequence in children's thinking about the past and how historians reconstruct the past and what the sequence means for teaching. In addition, researchers in the HE 3 tradition have conclusively demonstrated the limitations of the Piagetian-derived research that in the 1970s suggested that children and adolescents could not understand history. They have shown that even in the elementary grades students can, with appropriate teaching, work with historical data in more sophisticated ways than was once believed (though this would not have come as a surprise to Fred Morrow Fling, who said as much in the 1890s).[11] As a result, not the least of the attractions of HE 3 is the scope it offers for a more adventurous, and more empirically grounded, pedagogy than provided by HE 1 or even the more student-centred HE 2.

Besides educational theory and psychology, HE 3 also draws on developments in historiography, most notably the loosening (some would say the severing) of the connection between history and the nation-state that resulted from the so-called new social history of the 1960s and succeeding decades. This came about in four ways. First, social history displaced political-military-diplomatic history from its place at the top of the historiographical hierarchy. Second, the so-called history-from-below of women, workers, minorities, and others complicated the conventional nation-building narrative to the point that many historians concluded that a comprehensively authoritative story of the past was no longer possible (though this has not prevented them from writing such histories). Third, social history revealed some of the less salubrious doings of the nation-state, to the point that its critics accused it of substituting 'victimology' for history. Fourth, it historicized the concepts of nation and nationhood, so that they became objects of analysis rather than taken-for-granted frameworks for research. Furthermore, outside the world of education, the combined pressures of regionalism and globalization raised questions about the future of the nation-state as a form of political community, with some historians taking the long view and pointing out that the nation-state was a relatively recent and not necessarily long-lived form of political organization. In this context it is perhaps not surprising that something like HE 3 could appear.

The denationalization of historical research has been further hastened by the impact of postmodern theory on historiography. It is true that only a few historians have taken up postmodernism in any serious way but all have been affected by its questioning of traditional concepts of objectivity and its focus on the discursive nature of the discipline. Postmodernism's insistence that knowledge is power in action has drawn new attention to the ways in which history can be misused for political advantage. National history, in particular, can be a potent force for dividing the world into us and them, friends and enemies, and thus demonizing the 'other.' This is, of course, hardly a new discovery. Over eighty years ago H.G. Wells held historians and history teachers responsible for the First World War, arguing that it was made possible by the militarism and nationalism that resulted from their teaching of 'the poison called history.'[12] After a century of genocide, mass murder, and other horrors, we are perhaps more conscious than ever before of what can happen when history is exploited for political gain. The result of all these developments, in education, historiography, and the world at large, has been to cast doubt on the very concept of national history, and, as a consequence, HE 1 has lost ground to both HE 2 and HE3.

However, while it has lost ground, it has not withdrawn from the field. Recent surveys done by the Historica Foundation show that schools still teach the standard topics of Canadian history, though not necessarily in the old chronological, narrative style.[13] Indeed, according to these surveys there is a de facto national curriculum in place in Canadian schools, though its design and organization vary from province to province. One version of history education has not eclipsed the other two, nor can one be classed as residual, one as dominant, and one as emergent. Rather, all three coexist, often in the same classroom. Teachers tend to select what they need from each. For the most part, teachers are driven by what they see as the needs of their students, not by a vision of citizenship. For better or worse, they look for what will work in their classrooms with their students, be it a film, a video, a collection of primary sources, or some other form of teaching unit.

This coexistence of three competing approaches to history education, together with the debates to which they give rise, sparked the history wars of the 1990s as defenders of HE 1, in Canada and elsewhere, sought to turn back the encroachments of HE 2 and HE 3.[14] In part this was a turf war among historians, as political historians fought to resist the advance of their social history colleagues, accusing them of trivializing and fragmenting the discipline and of abandoning their responsibilities as public intellectuals. It was also a reaction to events in the wider society, which, in the case of Canada, included attempts at constitutional reform, the unfinished business of Quebec's place in Confederation, the demand of the First Nations for constitutional recognition, worries about the consequences of multiculturalism, the pressures of globalization, and the like – all of which raised questions about Canada's future and, by extension, its past, as people searched for historical precedents for their preferred policy choices. In fact, ever since the 1890s Canada has experienced a sense of crisis over the teaching of history once every generation: first in the 1890s, again in the 1920s, then in the 1940s, later in the 1960s, and again today. In every case the perceived crisis had more to do with fears for the future of the country than concern for what schools were or were not doing. And in every case the same concerns appeared: history was not sufficiently national; Quebec and English-speaking Canada were learning two different versions of history; students neither knew enough nor cared enough about history. The not-so-hidden assumption in every case was that if only the schools were to do a better job of teaching history, Canada would be safer and stronger.

It is not self-evident, however, that people who know history (including historians) are thereby better citizens than those who do not. Nor is it clear that an understanding of the past necessarily leads to a better understanding of the present. I spend most of my time with people who know less history than I do, but my judgments on current affairs are no more intelligent or perceptive than theirs. Of course, this might simply reveal my failings, but historians themselves are not conspicuous for their success as political analysts. Moreover, it is hardly unusual for equally expert historians, applying the same historical methods to the same historical phenomena, to arrive at different answers to the same questions.

At a less refined level, the mundane reality of many history classrooms belies the grandiose claims of history's supporters for its contribution to citizenship. For many students, history is simply one more hurdle to be cleared on the way to graduation. I once asked a Grade 10 class what they hoped to get out of Grade 10. The students told me that I had answered my own question: they hoped to get out of Grade 10. Why? So they could enter Grade 11, which they also hoped to get out of so that could enter Grade 12. And so on and so on. They saw their schooling for what it so easily becomes: a sorting and credentialing machine in which the accumulation of credits becomes the primary goal. Early in my teaching career, pressed for time and with no access to a duplicating machine, I spent three or four lessons dictating notes to a Grade 12 history class. This was something I rarely did, but the textbook was not very good, a provincial examination was looming, and I wanted to be sure that my students were ready for it. To my surprise, some of them told me they enjoyed the lessons. Their notebooks were full and their notes were well organized with the appropriate headings and sub-headings. Of course, their satisfaction might have been an indication that they were not all that impressed by my normal teaching, but I prefer to believe that my students saw things for what they were. Because the priority was to pass the examination, it made sense to prepare for it as efficiently and painlessly as possible.

Where, then, does all this leave us? What is, or should be, history education today? HE 1, HE 2, and HE 3 all have something to offer but none offers a completely satisfactory rationale that might convince policy makers, the public, and, not least, students, especially at a time when all three groups seem to value education primarily for its contribution to career preparation and the winning of competitive advantage over others. As a Quebec student asked a few years ago, 'A quoi me servir de savoir que des Français sont morts de scorbut pendant l'hiver de 1642? ... Certainement pas à me trouver une job!'[15] Unless we can answer this question in a way that students can understand, history teachers will always be working against the odds.

Above all, the case for compulsory history education must address two fundamental questions: What does the study of history contribute to the general education of students that no other subject can offer? Why should children and adolescents be compelled to study it? The answers to both questions can be found in a conception of history education that combines elements of HE 1, HE 2, and HE 3 into a new approach that I will call HE 4. In fact, it is not really new, as it reflects what good teachers have been doing for years and in many ways is simply an updating of precepts first enunciated some hundred years ago.

Though in recent years the nation-building narrative of HE 1 has fallen under something of a cloud, it still offers us three valuable lessons: 1) that narrative is an important part of history and can be a valuable way of presenting it; 2) that history education does not exist in a socio-political void; and 3) that knowledge (i.e., memorized knowledge of specific, facts, dates, events, and the like) matters.

Regardless of recent debates among historians and theorists about the nature and purpose of historical narrative and narrative history, HE 1 reminds us that, pedagogically speaking, narrative is a valuable, even an indispensable, tool for teaching history. Just as narrative history is the kind of history that most appeals to non-specialist adult audiences, so history-as-story has a particular appeal to children and adolescents. Moreover, history-as-story does not have to take the form of the traditional grand narrative, whose failings are described by Tim Stanley in chapter 3 of this volume. There are many ways to tell a story. A hundred years ago some history educators were describing ways of telling stories that in effect called on children to participate in the events the stories described, to describe them through the eyes of different characters in the story, to second guess those characters, to halt the narrative flow and speculate where the story might go next, and to provide alternative endings.[16] Stories can obviously be told from different points of view. They even can be told deconstructively so that their use of evidence, their assumptions, and their rhetorical strategies are made apparent.

Nor does history-as-story inherently or necessarily entail a view of history as the authoritative transmission of a single, uncontested view of the past. A story can raise more questions than it answers. Narrative history is not necessarily opposed to analytical history, or to *histoire-problème*, for example. Narrative can be a useful way to illuminate an analysis or unravel a problem for the uninitiated reader. This is, in fact, a large part of the appeal of micro-history: it tells a more or less linear story, usually of a specific person in a specific place coping with a specific experience, while also making clear the evidence on which the story is based and how it has been used, and locating the story itself in a wider temporal and cultural context. To take only three well-known examples, Carlo Ginzburg's *The Cheese and the Worms*, Angela Bourke's *The Burning of Bridget Cleary*, and Robert Bartlett's *The Hanged Man* all present us with an enthralling narrative organized around a central character and a dominant event while also giving us an equally enthralling and transparent account of how the authors used their evidence to construct and interrogate the story they have to tell.

HE 1 also reminds us that history education is not an abstract intellectual exercise but exists in the specific context of schooling, and that schooling, no matter what its degree of autonomy, is at root an instrument of public policy and collective aspiration, which are themselves the site of tension and disagreement. In Canada, for example, history education takes place in a Canadian context, regardless of whether one sees Canada as a nation or a bi-national, or for that matter a multi-national, state. Indeed, the teaching of history provides a useful vehicle for introducing students to the whole debate over the nature of Canada as a political community. There are those who say that this debate in fact constitutes the essence of Canada, that Canada is a continuing conversation among its citizens as to what kind of society they see themselves as living in and how they hope to shape it. To the extent that this is so, it makes it even more imperative to put students in a position where they will be able to contribute to the conversation, and to do this successfully they need to know and understand Canada's history.

It does not seem particularly contentious to require children and adolescents to study the history (and the debates that surround it) of the country in which they are growing up to become citizens. More than in most countries, Canada's most pressing contemporary problems are the product of its history. Indeed, Canada's history has made it a country that is markedly different from the conventional Euro-American conception of the nation-state, and this places particular demands on its citizens, although both Europe and the United States are now gingerly travelling along the trail that Canada first blazed and continues to explore, as they seek ways to accommodate linguistic and cultural diversity and to reconcile claims of personal identity with the demands of statehood. Jürgen Habermas, for example, has argued for what he calls 'constitutional patriotism' as the keystone of German unity and identity.[17] It is something that Canada was exploring as early as Confederation itself. If it is to prove successful, whether in Germany, Canada, or anywhere else, it demands citizens who are historically informed.

In other words, schools must introduce their students to what might loosely be called the 'big picture' of Canada's history. In the particular situation of Canada, it is difficult to see where else they will get it if not in schools. This does not require us to return to the largely outdated and discredited nation-building narrative that characterized HE 1, though many of the traditional landmarks will remain, albeit it with some reconstruction. Some will be open to interpretation, as when Quebec history curricula treat the Act of Union of 1840 as a major dividing line in Canada's history, as opposed to English Canada's choice of 1867, or as when women's historians observe that nothing changed in women's lives in 1867 and that the birth control pill might be more important than the British North America Act in the history of Canadian women. Some old landmarks will be rebuilt – for example, as the Proclamation of 1763 comes to be seen as being as important in the history of the First Nations as it is in the history of English-French relations. Some markers might well be abandoned altogether and others added. For example, HE 1 treated the years from the 1890s to the 1910s in terms of three major developments: the European settlement of the Prairies, French-English relations, and the slow progression towards autonomy in international affairs. By the 1980s, however, this narrative had shifted to include, and often to emphasize, the political and social consequences of the rapid industrialization and urbanization that characterized these years.

In short, to suggest that history education in schools should still embrace a narrative of Canada's historical trajectory is not to call for a return to the exclusionary nation-building narrative of a generation ago, with all its claims of definitiveness and authority. It is, rather, to introduce students to the evolution of the country in which most of them will become adult citizens. Just as most of us would not buy a house or a car without knowing something of its history, its strengths and weaknesses, its repair record, the reputation of its maker, and so forth, so the exercise of citizenship depends in part on our understanding of the state and society of which we are citizens. Citizens do not create a country from scratch. They inherit one that has been shaped over time, repaired and remodelled, patched here and renovated there, and that has developed its share of foibles and idiosyncrasies, some of which can no doubt be fixed but many of which simply have to be lived with. If nothing else, citizenship is a historically entrenched phenomenon.

In the case of Canada, this historically informed view of citizenship places a particular responsibility on the schools. Although we gain our understanding of the past from a variety of sources, we get our first, and for many of us often our only, systematic introduction to the history of Canada as a whole in school. In countries such as England, France, the United States, and many others, everyday life is replete with references to the national past, whether in advertising, popular entertainment, television sitcoms, pop music, news reporting, or a variety of other forms. In Canada, at least outside Quebec, there are few such references. Canadian culture is remarkably devoid of historical reference at the level of everyday life; most Canadians are likely to see far more American than Canadian or international references in their daily lives. This is perhaps why Canadians so frequently express their surprise when, as adults, they find Canadian history interesting. Even Mark Starowicz, the producer of the well-received television series *Canada: A People's History,* reported his amazement at the sheer drama of Canada's history though the series revealed little that was not already known to anyone who had kept up with the work of Canada's historians. The problem is that Canada has very few avenues by which this work can reach a wider audience, which again places a particular responsibility on the schools, not simply to teach students how to make sense of contemporary problems, as in HE 2, or think historically, as in HE 3, but to give them the historical knowledge they are unlikely to find anywhere else.

Even in its heyday, HE 1 was often criticized for turning history into a long and tedious march across deserts of facts and dates. As a result, the rejection of HE 1 that set in by the 1970s led to a more general rejection of the value of factual knowledge. There is a long tradition in educational theory, dating back at least to Socrates, that 'knowing how' is more important than 'knowing that' – in other words that skills and ways of thinking are more valuable than memorized knowledge. In some ways, of course, they obviously are. One of educationists' favourite maxims is that it is better to teach someone how to fish than to give them fish ready to eat. Perhaps so, but the two are not mutually exclusive, and, if I were starving, I would appreciate being given some fish before receiving any lessons in how to catch them. Nonetheless, the dichotomy between knowledge and skills (or product and process, in the jargon of edu-speak) remains strong. In recent years the appearance of the Internet and computerized databases has made it even more rigid. Employers and educationists alike argue that we no longer need to teach facts but only how to access them, and schools increasingly concentrate on such generic skills as problem solving, decision making, critical thinking, meta-cognition, and even entrepreneurialism.

Such a focus makes a certain sense from an employer's point of view. It is not difficult to see why an employer might want workers with plenty of skills but little general knowledge. With skills, workers know how to do their jobs. Without knowledge, they have no basis for questioning anything. George Orwell gave us a chilling picture of workers like this in his description of the Ministry of Truth in *Nineteen Eighty-Four*. There he described men and women who enjoyed the intellectual challenge of rewriting the past and converting literature into Newspeak but who never thought to ask why they were doing it or what the consequences of their work might be. Indeed, their lack of knowledge made such questions meaningless to them. The exception, of course, was Orwell's central character, Winston Smith. And it was Winston's knowledge, not his skills, that got him into trouble, for he knew just enough to suspect that the way things were was not the way they had always been and therefore necessarily had to be. In the same way, if we are arguing with a Holocaust denier, we cannot break off the argument in order to rush to a computer to access some convenient web site. We need the relevant knowledge in our heads, not just at our fingertips. Obviously, we cannot know all that we need to know. We cannot even be certain what it is that we need to know. And we forget much of what we are taught in school. To this extent, the skills mongers have a point. But this does not mean that knowledge does not matter. The very least that school can do is to give students the broad, more or less systematic, knowledge of the past that they will not get anywhere else, no matter how much they watch the History Channel.

All this ought to be so obviously banal as not to be worth saying, were it not for the tendency in some discussions of history education (one sees it in some, though not all, versions of HE 3, for example) to treat the acquisition of knowledge as merely instrumental or incidental to some other purpose. Even the most committed advocates of HE 3 allow that historical thinking cannot be mastered without knowledge, but some of them seem prepared to treat knowledge simply as a means to an end, and therefore select whatever knowledge they deem most useful for teaching students to think historically. My argument, by contrast, is that not all historical knowledge is equal, that some kinds of historical knowledge are more important than others, and that, in the context of educating the young for citizenship in Canada, a broad general knowledge of Canadian and world history is of particular importance.

Its view of knowledge limits the value of HE 2, which turns to history primarily for the elucidation (and, in some of its more naively utopian versions, even the solution) of contemporary problems and 'public issues.' The strength of HE 2 lies in its reminder that a knowledge of the past can help us understand the problems of the present, even if this understanding often means learning to live with them rather than to 'solve' them (which is perhaps a particularly useful lesson in the Canadian context). Its weakness is that in doing so it makes the past too much the prisoner of the present. It is true, as the philosopher Benedetto Croce once observed, that all history is contemporary history, but this is different from valuing only those aspects of the past that are believed to speak most directly to the concerns of the present. In my own teaching I often found my high school students to be especially receptive to what might be called the pastness of the past, its difference and remoteness from the present, so that the study of history became a form of time travel. The very foreignness of the past helped it to illuminate the taken-for-grantedness of the present. The problem is not that HE 2 disparages or devalues knowledge, or even that it treats it selectively (for selection is inevitable), but that its principle of selection is too restrictive. What matters about the past is not so much what is important to us but what was important to it. Moreover, in its concern with public issues and contemporary problems, and with the teaching of concepts and themes, HE 2 inevitably absorbs history into an interdisciplinary social studies in which it loses not only its curricular distinctiveness but also its disciplinary integrity. It treats the past as a treasure trove of case studies, examples, and precedents, thereby robbing it of the contextual coherence that makes it intelligible.

This, of course, is what HE 3 sets out to remedy. No one can reasonably deny HE 3's claim that what it variously calls historical thinking or historical consciousness is both an important educational goal and a valuable element of democratic citizenship. The proponents of HE 3 make a persuasive case when they argue that we cannot separate the teaching and learning of history from an understanding of the nature of history as a discipline, of the distinction between the past and history, of the nature of historical evidence, of the relationship between objectivity and interpretation, of the criteria that distinguish better interpretations from worse, and so forth. But this is not enough. The weakness of HE 3 lies in its attitude to knowledge, which it variously ignores, takes for granted, or treats as instrumental to the attainment of historical thinking. It accepts the obvious reality that historical thinking cannot occur in a vacuum, that students must think historically about something, but it tends to treat that something as whatever is best suited to help students think. It is largely silent on the question of whether, as I am arguing here, knowledge is an important component of citizenship and, if so, whether some kinds of knowledge are therefore more important than others.

This is why I find myself drawn to the idea of historical mindedness as it was understood in the 1890s. It lies at the centre of HE 4. Historical thinking and, to some extent, historical consciousness describe the professional mindset of the historian, the skills, habits of mind, and disciplinary norms involved in the study of history. Historical-mindedness, by contrast, describes the way of viewing the world that the study of history produces. It is a compound of knowledge, skills, and habits of mind. It is the result of the enlargement of experience that arises from the study of other times and other places. It is the ability to situate the immediate concerns of the present in some kind of comparative perspective and to see the world as it appears to others. It helps us understand ourselves as the inheritors of the past and the legatees of the future. It is a composite of HE 1's concern for narrative, context, and knowledge; of HE 2's use of history for the understanding of the present and its concentration on skills, concepts, and problems; and of HE 3's emphasis on the importance of history as a form of disciplined inquiry. It even accommodates the postmodern insistence on the fundamentally interpretative nature of history and its dangerous potential for putting knowledge at the service of power.

How, then, to translate all this into terms that would make sense to the Quebec student, and many others like him, who wondered how knowing that people died of scurvy in 1642 would help him in life, and not least in getting a job? Perhaps the first step is simply to discuss with students why it is useful for them to study history, since such research as we have suggests that this does not happen as often as one might think. In my own teaching, I found three arguments to be the most useful when discussing the value of history with students.

One is to put aside the utilitarian arguments for history and to show that it is interesting, even fun, as entertaining as any film or novel and in many ways more gripping, as it deals with what has actually happened and how we find out about it. Obviously, this is much more a matter of demonstration than exhortation. A teacher's declaration that history is interesting is unlikely to convince students. They have to find it out for themselves. Traditionally, this has led teachers to look for such exotica as John A. Macdonald's drinking habits or Mackenzie King's communing with spirits as a way of adding human interest to the story of the past. Many teachers have their personal files of anecdotes, eye-witness accounts, scandals, and the like with which to regale their students. Not the least of the pedagogical attractions of the *Dictionary of Canadian Biography* is its making this kind of information available to a general readership. The problem with this approach, however, is its not-so-hidden message that 'real' history is so dull that it needs to be enlivened in this way.

In my experience, the most effective way to arouse students' interest in history is to present it in the form of problems that they can explore, thereby countering its tendency to become a form of recitative memory work. This can be done in two ways. One is to do everything possible to portray the people of the past as facing problems whose outcome they could not foretell with the limited and incomplete information at their disposal, and inevitably operating within the confines of the conventional wisdom of their culture. In short, history becomes a study of human agency. This entails abandoning the stance of the retrospective and omniscient narrator whose function is to tell the story of what actually happened in the past, while also passing judgment on it, outlining five causes of this and seven results of that, noting that such and such was predictable or even inevitable, thus turning history into an exercise in retrodiction. Instead, it means trying to see the people of the past through their own eyes, telling their stories as they experienced them (so far as this is at all possible), looking towards an unknown and uncertain future while struggling to cope with the demands of their living present. There is nothing in Canadian or any other history that cannot be taught in this way, whether it be the high politics of Confederation or the everyday life of those involved in the fur trade. The second way to inject a sense of problem into history, and thereby to arouse students' interest, is to adopt the pedagogy favoured by HE 3 and introduce students to problems of evidence and interpretation. One might, for example, require them to write history from primary sources for themselves, or introduce them to such standard historiographical issues as the impact of the Conquest on New France or the compact theory of Confederation, or engage them in genuinely open-ended historical puzzles of the sort designed by Ruth Sandwell and John Lutz in their series of *Great Unsolved Mysteries in Canadian History*, or invite them to join with their teachers in making sense of historical data, as described by Chad Gaffield in chapter 6 of this volume.

The second argument for the importance of history is more utilitarian. I used to tell my students that it provided them with a form of intellectual self-defence. Adapting a phrase from Trotsky, who during the Russian Civil War once told a sceptical audience that they might not be interested in war, but war was certainly interested in them, I used to tell my students that though they might not be interested in history, history was most certainly interested in them. They were the prisoners of the past in ways they did not even realize, and what they did not know could hurt them. This argument for history as self-defence can be developed in at least seven ways. First, history armours us against all those people who claim to know it and are only too anxious to tell us what it proves. Second, it releases us from the grip of the past, which so easily holds us captive and shapes our ideas. Third, it teaches us how to be constructively sceptical (but not cynical or blindly rejectionist) when faced with appeals and arguments. Fourth, it protects us from being misled by the taken-for-granted conventional wisdom of our own times. Fifth, by showing us a wide variety of alternative belief systems, social practices, cultural norms, and the like, it enlarges our awareness of alternatives and choices. Sixth, it helps us understand and take part in the debates that are going on around us about the the future of Canada and of the world more generally, debates that are going to affect us whether we like it or not. And, finally, it makes us less short-sighted and narrow-minded than we would otherwise be by helping us situate the present in the context of the transition from past to future so that we are not governed solely by the short-term imperatives of the here and now. In my own teaching, I made liberal use of H.G. Wells's dictum to the effect that civilization is a race between education and catastrophe, adding that the study and teaching of history (on which in the 1920s Wells declared himself to be a 'fanatic') are crucial to education's victory.

The third argument I used with my students in defence of the study of history was that it enlarges our experience by showing us a wide range of human institutions and behaviour, thereby freeing us from the constraints of the present. To paraphrase the philosopher Isaiah Berlin, the best way to understand what human beings are capable of, both for good and ill, is to understand what they have done. History teachers are sometimes inclined to repeat Santayana's maxim that those who do not know the past are condemned to repeat it, but this is too simple. One could equally well argue that those who do know the past learn to repeat it even better the second time around. The point of learning about the past is to understand ourselves and our capabilities as historically situated beings. If the unexamined life is indeed not worth living, it is history that provides the best means of examination available to us. One of the descriptions of history teaching that most appeals to me is to be found in H.G. Wells's 1919 novel, *The Undying Fire*. Wells based his central character, Job Huss, on his friend Frederick Sanderson, a school principal whose reforming ways often created controversy. Under pressure for his innovations, Huss was comforted by a letter from a former student: 'You made us think and feel that the past of the world was our own history; you made us feel that we were in one living story with the reindeer men and the Egyptian priests, with the soldiers of Caesar and the alchemists of Spain; nothing was dead and nothing alien; you made discovery and civilization our adventure and the whole future our inheritance.'[18] This is an aspect of history education that is absent from HE 1, HE 2, and HE 3. Combined with a regard for the importance of historical method, it describes the historical mindedness that is the essence of what I propose as HE 4.

NOTES

1 George Orwell, *Nineteen Eighty-Four* (Harmondsworth: Penguin, 1954), 126–7. Subsequent page references are to this edition.
2 G. McDiarmid and D. Pratt, *Teaching Prejudice: A Content Analysis of Social Studies Textbooks Authorized for Use in Ontario: A Report to the Ontario Human Rights Commission* (Toronto: Ontario Institute for Studies in Education, 1971).
3 These reports are: National Council of Education, *Observations on the Teaching of History and Civics in Primary and Secondary Schools of Canada* (Winnipeg: National Council of Education, 1923); W.N. Sage, 'The Teach-

ing of History in the Elementary Schools of Canada,' Canadian Historical Association, *Report of the Annual Meeting Held at Montreal, May 23, 1930*, 55–63; Women's International League for Peace and Freedom, *Report of the Canadian School History Textbook Survey* (Toronto: WILPF, 1933); Canadian and Newfoundland Education Association, 'Report of the Committee for the Study of Canadian History Textbooks,' *Canadian Education* 1 (1945): 3–35; J. Katz, *The Teaching of Canadian History in Canada: A Survey Study of the Teaching of History in Junior and Senior High Schools* (Winnipeg: University of Manitoba Press, 1953); N. Frye, ed., *Design for Learning* (Toronto: University of Toronto Press, 1962); A.B. Hodgetts, *What Culture? What Heritage?* (Toronto: Ontario Institute for Studies in Education, 1968).

4 G. Grant, *Lament for a Nation: The Defeat of Canadian Nationalism* (Toronto: McClelland and Stewart, 1965); D.G. Creighton, *Canada's First Century, 1867–1967* (Toronto: Macmillan, 1970).

5 H. Neatby, 'Education for Democracy,' *Dalhousie Review* 24 (1944): 49; Katz, *The Teaching of Canadian History*, 31; William L. Morton, 'Preface,' in Katz, *Teaching of Canadian History*, 1.

6 The inspiration for the structure of the disciplines approach was J.S. Bruner, *The Process of Education* (Cambridge: Harvard University Press, 1960). For the public issues approach, see D. Oliver and J. Shaver, *Teaching Public Issues in the High School* (Boston: Houghton Mifflin, 1966) and its Canadian adaptation, P. Bourne and J. Eisenberg, *Social Issues in the Curriculum: Theory, Practice, and Evaluation* (Toronto: Ontario Institute for Studies in Education, 1978). For the 'new social studies' of the 1960s, see E. Fenton, *The New Social Studies* (New York: Holt, Rinehart and Winston, 1967); and E. Fenton, ed., *Teaching the New Social Studies in Secondary Schools* (New York: Holt Rinehart and Winston, 1968). The Canadian context is explored in K. Osborne, '"To the Schools We Must Look for Good Canadians": Developments in the Teaching of History in the Schools since 1960,' *Journal of Canadian Studies* 22 (1987): 104–26; and B. Davis, *Whatever Happened to High School History? Burying the Political Memory of Youth, Ontario, 1945–1995* (Toronto: Lorimer, 1995).

7 The best references here are C. Portal, ed., *The History Curriculum for Teachers* (London: Falmer, 1987); R. Martineau, *L'histoire à l'école, matière à penser ...* (Montreal: L'Harmattan, 1999); P. Stearns, P. Seixas, and S. Wineburg, eds., *Knowing, Teaching and Learning History: National and International Perspectives* (New York: New York University Press, 2000); S. Wineburg, *Historical Thinking and Other Unnatural Acts* (Philadelphia: Temple University Press, 2001); S.G. Grant, *History Lessons: Teaching, Learning, and Testing in U.S. History Classrooms* (Mahwah, NJ: Lawrence

Erlbaum, 2003); and J.-P. Charland, *Les élèves, l'histoire et la citoyenneté: Enquête auprès d'élèves des regions de Montréal et Toronto* (Quebec: Les Presses de l'Université Laval, 2003).

8 M.S. Barnes, *Studies in Historical Method* (Boston: Heath, 1896); F.M. Fling and H.W. Caldwell, *Studies in European and American History: An Introduction to the Source Study Method in History* (Lincoln, NE: Miller, 1897); M.W. Keatinge, *Studies in the Teaching of History* (London: A. & C. Black, 1910). For recent studies, see F.E. Monteverde, 'Considering the Source: Mary Sheldon Barnes,' in M.S. Crocco and O.L. Davis Jr., eds., *'Bending the Future to Their Will': Civic Women, Social Education and Democracy* (Lanham, MD: Rowman and Littlefield, 1999), 17–46; and K. Osborne, 'Fred Morrow Fling and the Source Method of Teaching History,' *Theory and Research in Social Education* 71 (2003): 466–501.

9 See the discussion and references in Wineburg, *Historical Thinking*, 37–60.

10 K. Egan, *Getting It Wrong from the Beginning: Our Progressivist Inheritance from Herbert Spencer, John Dewey, and Jean Piaget* (New Haven, CT: Yale University Press, 2002).

11 See, for example, J. Brophy and B. VanSledright, *Teaching and Learning History in Elementary Schools* (New York: Teachers College Press, 1997); and B. VanSledright, *In Search of America's Past: Learning to Read History in Elementary School* (New York: Teachers College Press, 2002).

12 H.G. Wells, *The Salvaging of Civilization: The Probable Future of Mankind* (New York: Macmillan, 1921), and his 'The Traveller Provokes His Old Friends, the Teachers, Again in a Paper Called "The Poison Called History"' in *Travels of a Radical Republican in Search of Hot Water* (Harmondsworth: Penguin Books, 1939), 89–121.

13 P. Shields and D. Ramsay, *Teaching and Learning about Canadian History across Canada* (Toronto: Historica Foundation, 2002); J.-P. Charland and S. Moisan, *L'enseignement de l'histoire dans les écoles françaises du Canada* (Toronto: Historica Foundation, 2003).

14 For the 1990s debates on the state of history in Canadian schools, see K. Osborne, '"Our History Syllabus Has Us Gasping": History in Canadian Schools – Past, Present, and Future,' *Canadian Historical Review* 81 (2000): 405–35; and K. Osborne, 'Teaching History in Schools: A Canadian Debate,' *Journal of Curriculum Studies* 35 (2003): 585–626.

15 'What use is it for me to know that the French died of scurvy in the winter of 1642? ... It certainly won't help me find a job.' M. Lachance, 'L'école: zéro en histoire,' *L'Actualité*, 1 March 1996, 34. A few years earlier a Newfoundland student posed a similar question: 'If I'm going to be a cop, why do I have to learn religion and history?' Quoted in W.D. Martin, *Student*

Views on Schooling in Newfoundland and Labrador (St. John's: Memorial University Faculty of Education, 1985), 64.

16 For an example of this approach, see C. McMurry, *Special Method in History* (New York: Macmillan, 1903).

17 For an explanation of the concept of constitutional patriotism, see Jürgen Habermas, *Between Facts and Norms: Contributions to a Discourse Theory of Law and Democracy* (Cambridge, MA: MIT Press, 1996), 491–515. For an informative review of the arguments for and against the concept, see Ciaran Cronin, 'Democracy and Collective Identity: In Defence of Constitutional Patriotism,' *European Journal of Philosophy* 11, no. 1 (2003): 1–28.

18 H.G. Wells, *The Undying Fire* (New York: Macmillan, 1919), 221.